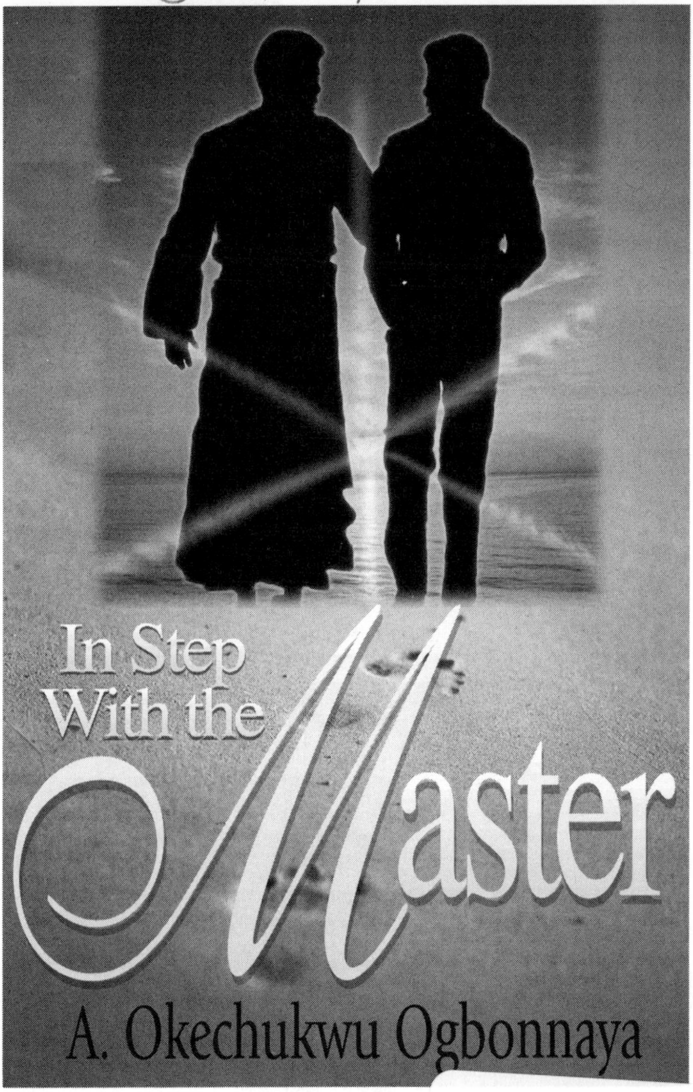

In Step With the Master

A. Okechukwu Ogbonnaya

Urban Ministries, Inc.
Chicago, IL

Publisher
Urban Ministries, Inc.
P.O. Box 463987
Chicago, IL 60643 6987

ISBN: 0-940955-53-9
Catalog 6-5110

Unless other wise noted, Scripture texts are taken fro the King James Version of the Bible.

DEDICATION

To Rev. Elliot Mason, an example of what
it means to follow Jesus.

CONTRIBUTIONS

My thanks to the following persons whose contributions enabled me to complete this work: Dr. Melvin Banks, founder/chairman Urban Ministries Inc., and Eric Wallace for their writing contributions; C. Jeff Wright, President UMI; the editorial staff: Kathryn Hall, Melody Jackson, Cheryl Wilson, Kim Brooks; and Denise Gates for copyediting this book.

TABLE OF CONTENTS

CHAPTER

FOREWORD

For those who seem to need complex interrelated systems in order to feel the power of what they know, the simplicity of the Gospel is unnerving. Ancient and modern philosophers have thrived in the creation of mazes of obtuse systems. Thus, we find that the simple Gospel appears mundane to the shallow and foolish, to the so-called learned. I have come to understand that the simplicity of the Gospels is what makes them profoundly deeper than the philosophical systems to which our world adheres.

We are called to embrace the Galilean simplicity from which flows the word of the Messiah. At the core of the call of the Gospel is the imperative to turn to divine simplicity. We are called to follow the one whose call to others contained no flowery rhetoric or complex versification but two words, "follow me." Whereas others philosophized about the nature of love, He simply loved. Where others wrote volumes on the art of healing, He simply healed. In doing the simple things and speaking simple words, Jesus transformed the world for all times.

Within this work we seek to examine some of those simple offerings of the Master to those who seek to follow Him. While this work does not claim to be a complete treatise on what it means to follow Jesus, it seeks to offer some thoughtful ideas about the act of following as demanded of every believer. For those who are looking for someone to lead them out of the quagmire of confusion and fruitless labor, we offer the simple words of the Master, "follow me." If you were already following the Master, it will not hurt to review the meaning of the call and how you have responded to it. For those who are searching for a way to belong in a world that excludes them, we say to you, "you are invited." For those who say, "now that I follow the Master I find myself in battles for which I seem to have no weapon

of defense," watch as the Master uses the Word to defeat the enemy. Know that the Word of God equips you. Listen as the Master says, "I give you authority over all the powers of the enemy." As you follow the Master you may find that sometimes you hurt physically, psychologically, or spiritually; hear the Messiah whisper to your soul, "you are made whole." These are some of the
ways in which I have sought to minister the simplicity of the Gospel within the pages of this book.

This book is a devotional that will help you in your daily study, as well as help your church community as they seek to grow in faith. Through these studies I hope the Lord will minister to you as much as the Spirit ministered to me in the process of putting these thoughts together.

The meaning of following in the steps of the Master is not merely a matter of youthful enthusiasm or mere idealistic dreams of disappointed old men. It is instead the resolve to be committed to God as the ultimate reality without whom one's life is meaningless. The one thing for which we as Christians (in the later part of this century) cannot be condemned for is following our Lord with excessive zeal or over commitment to the cause of our Lord. The questions that confront us are: Behind our religious jingles are there coins of spiritual value? Behind the passionate enthusiasm of so-called renewal movements, is there a redemptive pathos that seeks to follow the Master's footsteps? Behind the seriousness of our religious rituals is there really a spiritual gem? Unless there is a radical commitment to follow in the steps of our Lord, we will find ourselves languishing behind as the Spirit moves the world to a new day of the Saviour's power. As heirs of the prophetic impulse, embodied in Jesus as Messiah, we can only reach our true destiny if we decide to unequivocally follow. If we do not follow, we will find it difficult to be loyal to the lordship of God's Son. If we do not follow, it will not be easy for us to believe. Only in following do we grasp the dependability of God's promises. We may never gain the simple insight into God's grace or His choice of us unless we resolve to follow the Spirit wherever it leads. This book is meant to help strengthen our spiritual resolve to follow Jesus Christ the Lord. Let us strive to follow.

A. Okechukwu Ogbonnaya, Ph.D.

Chapter One

YOU ARE CALLED BY THE MASTER

Matthew 4:18-22

*And Jesus, walking by the sea of Galilee, saw two brethren, Simon called Peter,
and Andrew his brother, casting a net into the sea: for they were fishers. 19And he
saith unto them, Follow me, and I will make you fishers of men. 20And they
straightway left their nets, and followed him. 21And going on from thence, he saw
other two brethren, James the son of Zebedee, and John his brother, in a ship with
Zebedee their father, mending their nets; and he called them. 22And they immediately left the ship and their father, and followed him.*

Matthew 9:9

And as Jesus passed forth from thence, he saw a man, named Matthew, sitting at the receipt of custom: and he saith unto him, Follow me. And he arose, and followed him.

The two events cited above occur after the narration of Jesus' temptation. Several things have happened to Jesus. First, He has faced the challenge of the demonic attacks of the devil. He has been attacked physically, through hunger; psychologically, to self-aggrandizement and illusion leading to suicide; and spiritually to commit idolatry. Having tried Jesus in every aspect of His personality without success, the devil now turns to someone dear to Him. We read in Matthew 12 that "He heard that John had been cast into prison." This can be seen as another attempt of the enemy to lay a stumbling block on the path of Jesus in order to keep Him from following the call of

God upon His life. From the Christmas story, you may recall that John the Baptist was Jesus' cousin. Not only was he the cousin of Jesus, their lives were bound by the thread of prophetic fulfillment. In fact, John baptized Jesus and introduced His ministry to the world. By laying hands on someone whom Jesus loved, Satan thought that he would place a stumbling block in the path of Jesus and force Him away from following the calling of God in His life. Having just emerged successfully from the temptation in the wilderness and the temptation which John's problem may have caused, Jesus went to Galilee and began to preach. Note how even Jesus Himself, though being the Lord, follows John's footsteps by beginning the same way John began, saying, "Repent: for the kingdom of heaven is at hand" (Matthew 4:17). If we look closely at the background, we see that certain things are demanded of those who wish to follow God and His Christ. In this chapter we shall examine the concept of discipleship.

Answering the Call of the Master

We follow in response to Jesus' call, not to the call of human beings. Jesus was the One who called Peter, Andrew, and Matthew. In the first century, there were many messianic pretenders who sought followers among the people of Israel. Messiahs were rising up each day and promising people deliverance from the oppression of the Romans. People went out of their way to look for saviours, and many were disappointed. The spiritual hunger of the times allowed many to enter into magic, false religions and cults. Many followed magicians, some of whom promised that they could break the power of Rome by calling on spirits. Some of these charged exorbitant prices from anyone who wanted to become their disciple. Even for the disciples of Jesus, the question must have been, "With so many voices calling for my allegiance, who do I follow?" How did they know that the one who was calling them was authentic? The disciples heard Jesus' voice and they followed. In the midst of all these noises, the disciples still followed Jesus.

Following Jesus means hearing and listening to His voice. Those who follow Jesus have learned to distinguish His voice from that of false messiahs. Jesus Himself declares that His sheep hear His voice, follow Him and He gives them eternal life (John 10:3). The fact that many of us enjoy invitations, especially when they make us feel important, may cause us to listen to voices that are not from our Lord. Furthermore, when we are in vulnerable situations, we may tend to listen to voices that may not come from God. But we must be careful because the call we respond to affects the kind of relationships we keep and the kind of persons we become. Usually when we listen to a voice, it means that we have decided to follow the direction of that voice. It means that we are willing to sacrifice some of our ways of doing things. In order to follow the voice of the one who calls, we must at least be willing move from where we are. The same thing happened to the first people whom Jesus called to follow Him. When Jesus commanded Peter to follow Him and Peter listened, right then and there Peter gave up his right to insist on having things his own way although it took him a long time to realize this.

The voice of Jesus which calls us to follow Him runs contrary to the voices that we hear in the world. We must admit that sometimes it runs contrary to the voice of our own egos. But, if we are truly to follow the Master and to walk in step with Him, we must be willing to set aside even our own deepest sentiments. If we are not willing to do this, we must question whether we are true followers of Jesus. When Jesus calls us to follow Him, it is a complete call which is directed to our whole person. Jesus does not say to any of us, "All I want is for your mind alone or for your body alone to follow me!" He simply says, "Follow me." There is perfection in the voice which makes the call complete because He who calls is perfect. When we hear the voice of Jesus saying "Follow me," to attempt to follow Him with one foot in the world is not to follow Him. To do that is to fall into the sin of idolatry. Following in that way is to declare our autonomy from God. To follow in that way is to insist that we know of another voice which has the power to create and to deliver us in the same way as the "word which was in the beginning by whom all things were created."

If we listen to the voice of Jesus calling, we will see that Jesus means to transform our reality and create within us divine greatness. Oh, if only we are willing listen and to follow! If only we are willing to follow the voice of Jesus which says, "Follow me." The power of this voice can create a new value within our being. But to do this, we must realize that we do not call ourselves, for the power to call is not in us. We cannot follow ourselves, for that is a vicious cycle which leads nowhere. But to follow, we must listen to the voice of the divine Son of the Living God. It is true that sometimes the voices which call us are not mainly that of Jesus or that of the devil or that of other human beings, but voices of our own conceit and deception. The only voice to which we must listen and follow is the voice of the divine Son of God, even Jesus Christ. In His voice alone, we find light and life.

The call to follow Jesus is extended to ordinary, awkward, and imperfect people. So if you are one of those, Jesus is saying to you, "Follow me." You do not have to be someone spectacular to follow Him. You do not have to be highly educated to follow Jesus. Throughout the centuries there have been two extreme arguments about people who are called to follow Jesus. Some have maintained that only the ignorant can successfully follow Jesus, while others have insisted that only those with deeper philosophical knowledge can follow. But we who have come to know Him understand that one does not have to be ignorant or highly educated to follow. Jesus is calling us, whoever we are, saying, "Follow me." Peter, Andrew, James, and John were ordinary fishermen whom Jesus called to be His followers (Matthew 4:19, 21). Peter, Andrew, James, John, and Matthew understood that they were not called because they were so special but because God loved them and was willing to let them walk with the Son. Matthew 9:9 indicates that Matthew was called from being a tax collector, a job the Jewish people loved to despise, yet the Master came to him and said simply, "Follow me." Tax collectors were local men of wealth who contracted with their city or district to collect taxes for Rome. They agreed to collect a certain amount and anything over belonged to them. In His mercy, Jesus said to Matthew, "Follow me." Peter, Andrew, James, and John were fishermen. Fishermen were considered honest laborers while tax collectors were considered dishonest and corrupt; yet to both, Jesus said, "Follow me."

Whether we belong to a system which abuses or to a group of people who have been abused, Jesus says, "Follow me." Jesus does not force people to follow Him; He simply calls all to follow Him. He does not disgrace people by shaming them into following Him; He simply says, "Follow me." Jesus led men and women to follow Him simply by calling them. Imagine the power of His words as He simply said, "Follow me." Imagine Him calling you today, "Follow me." With these few words, the Lord transformed the life of ordinary fishermen, tax collectors, political zealots, religious conservatives, and liberals alike. But what does it mean to follow Him? What does it mean to follow the Lord and Saviour of the world? "Follow me." Oh, how these words must have stirred the souls of those who first heard them spoken from the lips of the Divine One! "Follow me." Oh, how it stirs my soul now. My Master, my soul responds, "Ah, my Lord. Yes, my Lord."

"Follow Me" Means Sacrifice

Sacrifice does not mean that we must do something to be saved. Rather, in the very act of following, we give up something of the world. It does cost us to follow Jesus (Luke 9:57-62). Cost is a faith issue. To make a sacrifice, we must possess some form of faith in the one who calls. Consider the sacrifices Peter, Andrew, James, and John were called to make in order to follow Jesus (Matthew 4:20, 22). They were being called to make a total life commitment which affected their social, economic, and, in fact, religious status. Each one of us who desires to follow Jesus must examine what it is that Christ expects us to give up in order to effectively follow Him. What we are willing to give up as we follow Him shows how deeply we are willing to be involved with the One who calls. We must give up our unbelief and follow. For many of us, following Jesus has meant a sacrifice of personal achievements and worldly ambitions. For others, it has meant a sacrifice of headstrong ignorance. Some followers of Jesus have had to sacrifice friends and even family for the sake of the kingdom of God. Such people who follow Jesus, even in the midst of immense loss, seem to understand that Jesus' call requires a complete and total surrender. They seem to understand that to gain Jesus is to gain the universe. In interpreting this passage, the church father Augustine states that "Christ is either Lord of all, or He is not Lord at all." We learn from the call of the disciples that this call is intensely personal. The disciples did not stop to ask another if it was all right for them to follow Jesus in response to His call. In the innermost core of their beings, they heard a voice calling in gentleness and power. They knew it was for them, so they followed.

These disciples were being called to follow faithfully. We are called to follow faithfully. Faithful following implies the willingness to obey Christ's commands. Jesus Himself said, "You are my disciples (followers) if you keep my commandments" (John 8:31). If, indeed, Jesus is God as we claim, our following must be wholehearted, with all our mind and strength. It also means that we must actively seek to eliminate those things which serve to hinder our authentic following of Christ from our way of living. There is a sense in which we must commit, moment-by-moment, to be followers of Jesus today, this week, this month, and this year. Placing ourselves on the altar is a daily activity. In the Gospel of Luke, Jesus said, "If any man will come after me, let him deny himself, and take up his cross daily, and follow me" (Luke 9:23). Although Luke is the only Gospel which adds "daily," it tells us of the perpetuity of this following.

"Follow Me" Means Purpose

In the call to follow Jesus is the declaration of purpose, "I will make you fishers of men." One of the most common ways to earn an honest living along the sea of Galilee was to fish. Here, we see Jesus walking along the shoreline where He encounters two brothers, Peter and Andrew, fishing. It is in the context of this activity that Jesus invited them to follow Him. His announcement that He would make them fishers of men is not surprising to the brothers. Though they may not have understood what it meant to be "fishers of men" (Matthew 4:19), they got the basic idea. To them, it must have been clear that their work was now to concentrate on human beings. It must have been clear to them that they were to bring human beings from the depth of darkness to a marvelous light. Jesus was not calling them to be spectators. Note that Jesus did not say that they were to watch Him be the fisher of men but that they were being called to be actively engaged in the task of wooing and convincing human beings to come out of the storm into the calm. The calling of the Lord comes with an implicit promise of the power to accomplish that purpose. "I will make you" is a solemn promise grounded in the nature of the divine. To follow Jesus the Master is to agree that He, as Lord, can make you into whatever God wills. Whenever God says "I will," there is a power within that word a creative movement coming from the very heart of God. The purpose for which God calls us is good. We who follow Jesus must always keep before us a question of purpose. The question for you and I may be: "What is God's will for me? What is the purpose of my calling? How must I follow Jesus in order to fulfill the purpose of my high calling?"

We Must Follow Jesus Immediately

How did Simon and Andrew respond to Jesus' call? (Matthew 4:19) Peter and Andrew left what they were doing and followed Jesus. The Greek word translated "left" carries the idea of abandoning someone or something. The response was the same when Jesus encountered James and John mending their nets with their father. Jesus saw them, then invited them and they responded by leaving their father to follow Him. In each of these cases, Matthew uses the word "immediately" to indicate that there was no delay in their action. The Greek word *eutheos* **(yoo-theh'-oce)** has a certain sense of urgency in it. We are not allowed to procrastinate. It means that they followed Jesus directly; they did not attempt to go around the command to follow. No delay tactics. They did not say, "My fellow fisherman are looking. What will they say?" Here they are being called to be creative agents within the reign of God. This word "immediately" has serious consequences for those of us who must follow the reign of God through Jesus Christ. It speaks to the radical transformation of value held by Peter and the disciples. Through their response, God speaks to us in our current situation. Our generation is often accused of being in a hurry. We are often called "the instant generation." We seem to be in a hurry but not in the right direction. We want to do many things immediately but following in the footsteps of the Master does not seem to be one of them. When it comes to the things of God, many of us go round and round, hoping that we can wear God down by our delays. By following the Lord immediately, the disciples rendered their everyday life under subjection to the spiritual ideal whose content shone forth through the voice of Jesus Christ. "Immediately" speaks to the fact that Peter and the disciples understood that no divinely ordained end is achieved by supposing that the call of God can be made secondary to any other call in life. "Immediately" also speaks to the inner orientation of those who are called. The ideal creative power which proceeds from God was already working in their lives and not even their economic considerations could stand in the way of their commitment to God's call through Jesus Christ. There must not be anything or anyone who can take the place of our primary commitment to follow Jesus. If we give priority to anyone else, then our willingness to follow Jesus is called into question. This call to follow Jesus' image should be our example as we seek to follow Him. Jesus' intense following of His call and the voice of the Father serves as our perpetual paradigm.

The word "immediately" speaks to the urgency of answering the call of the Lord. Why must we respond immediately? The Scriptures are quite clear about the urgent nature of the call of the Gospel. Jesus Himself began His proclamation with the words, "The kingdom of heaven is at hand," which could be paraphrased to say "The kingdom of God is coming quickly." The Bible is fond of using the word "today" to emphasize the need to obey the voice of God immediately (Psalm 95:7-8; Hebrews 3:7, 13, 15; 4:7). When one understands the urgency of following Jesus, then one begins to understand the urgency of calling others also to follow. The dying world will not wait. Why should we wait? Why should we delay following the Master who is able to save the world from death?

"Follow Me" Means Obedience

Christ calls upon us, His people, to hear and follow His voice. We call Him Master, or Lord or Saviour; then let us be His willing, obedient people. Let us hear the voice of His teaching, of his love, and in both, let us hear His Spirit. Let us hear and heed. Let us hear and yield. Let us hear and follow. The Master's voice must be heard today. The Saviour's footsteps must be followed today. This day of opportunity will not last always. Step up while "it is called today." Hearing the voice of Christ is the same as believing. Hear. Believe. Follow. May the Lord keep us from hardness of heart which, at rock bottom, is distrust in the Lord. The sins of humanity from Adam to Israel have been an unwillingness to tread in the steps of the Lord. The murmurings of Israel should warn us of the danger in refusing to follow. We are admonished to follow our God. God's calling is not subject to human passions or an emotional roller-coaster. Refusing to walk in step with the Lord is evil. If we walk in our own way, then we deserve the results which are pronounced in the Scriptures. But if we walk in the steps of the Lord our God, we are assured of God's promises. Let us be aware of the voice of the Master in our hearts, let us follow with humility. Lead us, O Lord, in your wondrous path. May we never stray from you. For you are our sovereign Lord. If we follow faithfully, there is a rest ordained for us. There is an everlasting refreshment in this life and in the life to come for those who follow. God's rest awaits those who in humility have chosen to follow in the footsteps of the Master. Jesus calls to you, me, and all who will hear saying, "Follow me" into rest and life.

Following Leads to Completeness

As Christians, we find completeness following our Master and Saviour. Followers of Jesus are not just ones who follow haphazardly; they must be intent on having their character trained to obey the signals of the Spirit. To say that the Christian is complete does not mean that we are perfect but that we are ones who move according to what the Greek New Testament calls "telos." It means that we are oriented toward maturity. Thus we have learned as the followers of Jesus to depend on the inner direction of His voice. We have learned, by grace not to be satisfied with stereotypical religion or so-called normal satisfaction with the typical piety of our world. As followers, we learn to never shut off our spiritual radar which directs us to the image of Christ. Although we must put every effort toward becoming mature, we must also remember that our maturity is ultimately determined by God who calls us and whom we follow. Often as followers of Jesus, we may face a deep sense of apathy and lack of spiritual drive which sometimes may be rooted in a sense of spiritual pride. In this case, we may be misled to believe that we have already achieved rather than "pressing on toward the mark of the high calling of Christ" (Philippians 3:12-14). Many of us who are believers of Jesus suffer from too much compliance and too little spiritual drive, and this is apathy covered by our monotonous religious activities. However, to move toward maturity, we must not focus on the sickness of other Christians nor our own sin sickness, we must stay focused on Jesus Christ and the

wholeness which He promises in order to grow (Ephesians 4:15). An amazing thing about following Jesus is that the One whom we follow is also the One who helps us in our pursuit. He is the beginning and the end of our quest. He is the beginning and the end of the journey.

In each case when Jesus called people to follow Him, He noticed them as persons in their own right. He then invited them to "follow" Him. In each case, the disciples left everything to follow Jesus. We each must make this decision as a responsible person. It does not matter what one's occupation is, whether a respected fisherman or a despised tax collector, the message is clear: Jesus is the one who initiates the call to discipleship and a disciple must be willing to leave all to follow Him. He or she must be willing to abandon their former way of life. Those who accept this challenge become witnesses to and participants in the "kingdom of God." They become fellow ministers of the Gospel with Jesus and true "fishers of men." They become kingdom persons because they have personally responded to the call of the Master.

As followers in the steps of Jesus, we are emancipated from the bondage of worldliness. By the fact that we have been chosen to follow Jesus, we rise through the power of His voice. The voice that calls us to follow is interested in the ultimate expansion of our horizons spiritually, psychologically, and physically. In this state of being called, there arises an intense devotion to the One who calls. This sense of devotion leads us to disassociate ourselves from all which may serve to hinder us from obeying the call to be a follower of Jesus Christ (Hebrews 12:1). As followers, we are now committed body and soul. We are not ruled by the "flesh," as Paul puts it. The state of true following is that of peace, where we as followers, are assured of the presence of the One who calls us. Those of us who are on this journey now know that though we may not be whole in ourselves, by responding to the call of the divine voice, we have been made complete in Christ. Thus, no power in the world can overcome those of us who have decided to follow the call to discipleship. In the past, before we answered this call to be in step with Jesus, little things may have easily derailed us. Now, looking into the face of the Master and following in His footsteps, we feel that we are secure in His shadow. Because we are made secure in that image, we may shake, but our foundation remains forever secure. To remain secure, we must continually give up the things that cause us to stray from the way of the Lord, including the spiritual delinquency and psycho-spiritual distortions which were rooted in our former ways of doing things. We must come under the lordship of Jesus. We must submit all our ways to the transforming power of Jesus Christ. His presence must become so intimately connected with who we are that, indeed, we are expression of His image as He is the expression of the image of God. We may still be concerned with the crisis of the social and economic roller-coaster in which we live. Yet our comprehension of the power of God working in our lives through Jesus Christ re-directs our gaze. The god of this world does not blind us any longer to the glorious light of the eternal God (2 Corinthians 4:4).

We must also cease from being second-generation followers. Most of us regard following Jesus as something that we inherit from our parents, hence our Christianity is vicarious Christianity. In fact, some of our church experiences predispose us to a vicarious experience with Jesus and as a result some fail to go directly to God for guidance or to seek a direct and immediate experience of the divine. Some live by the experience of others and truly believe that this is the way to follow Jesus. This kind of following makes for insecure and maladjusted Christians. Excessive exposure to others and to the ways of the world rather than a radical openness to the image of Jesus leaves too many of us spiritually unhealthy and causes us to be shaky followers. But emancipation from this mode of Christian existence must come from transparent living in the presence of God without pretense and without covering. God alone through the power of the Son, Jesus Christ working by the power of the Holy Spirit can readjust us to the divine image thereby setting us free. Those who are following Jesus understand the effect of this emancipating power. They know the reality of the lives of those who leave all to follow Jesus. Such emancipative following is not just a private thing but a public declaration of divine purpose which manifests itself in public witness in the lives of others. Though one used to live an enclosed life full of lies, one now lives in the truth. Though one used to live a life of bondage, one moves into a life of freedom open, liberated, and focused in the light which is Jesus, the Son of God. Since only those who follow Jesus experience this emancipating power, the believer cannot blame others for not being free. It is impossible for anyone else to take the blame for your failure to experience the freedom of salvation complete emancipation which is offered to those who choose to follow Jesus. If they follow faithfully, those who walk with Jesus on the dusty road can look back and see their chains falling as they follow. If you want to experience emancipation, all you have to do is "follow." We may be able to blame society for many of the things that happen to us, but the blame for failing to choose to be salvifically free cannot be laid at any other's doorstep but that of our own will. We must be willing to leave our chains psychological, spiritual, physical, and otherwise to follow Jesus. The problems of our failure to follow are not resolved by blaming the church, the pastor, the deacon, the choir, or even the ushers. These people may and can be real problems in our way as we seek to follow Jesus. Even the devil may work against us. But no one has the power keep us away from God nor what God offers us in the way of freedom. If you follow Jesus, emancipation is yours. We must all say daily with the singer:

I have decided to follow Jesus.
I have decided to follow Jesus.
I have decided to follow Jesus.
No turning back,
No turning back.

Though no one joins me, still I will follow.
Though no one joins me, still I will follow.
Though no one joins me, still I will follow.
No turning back,
No turning back.

The Cross before me, the world behind me.
The Cross before me, the world behind me.
The Cross before me, the world behind me.
No turning back,
No turning back.

Do not be afraid to follow when God calls you. God has promised to give us guidance for the journey (Numbers 9:15;10:10). There are several promises in Scripture that tell us that God will guide us (Psalm 25:9; 32:8; 48:14). Our maturity depends upon our listening to Jesus and focusing on Him. We follow Jesus, not as the crowd in the Gospel of John which followed mainly for the bread which perishes. We follow not because the crowd thinks it is fashionable. Rather, we follow intentionally and decisively, even when it means going against the crowd. We must trust in the inner guidance of the Spirit which proceeds from the One who calls to us and lead us in our walk with the Lord. Let us follow Jesus; He is calling us now. If we keep in step with the Master, we will inherit life. Let us follow! Let our heartfelt prayer be: Oh Master, let me walk with Thee. Oh Master, my all in all, let me follow you! I will gladly give my all. Yes, my very life. Let me follow You and keep in step with You my Lord.

Chapter Two

BY THE WORD YOU ARE EQUIPPED

Matthew 4:1-11

Then was Jesus led up of the Spirit into the wilderness to be tempted of the devil. [2]And when he had fasted forty days and forty nights, he was afterward an hungered. [3]And when the tempter came to him, he said, If thou be the Son of God, command that these stones be made bread. [4]But he answered and said, It is written, Man shall not live by bread alone, but by every word that proceedeth out of the mouth of God. [5]Then the devil taketh him up into the holy city, and setteth him on a pinnacle of the temple, [6]And saith unto him, If thou be the Son of God, cast thyself down: for it is written, He shall give his angels charge concerning thee: and in their hands they shall bear thee up, lest at any time thou dash thy foot against a stone. [7]Jesus said unto him, It is written again, Thou shalt not tempt the Lord thy God. [8]Again, the devil taketh him up into an exceeding high mountain, and sheweth him all the kingdoms of the world, and the glory of them; [9]And saith unto him, All these things will I give thee, if thou wilt fall down and worship me. [10]Then saith Jesus unto him, Get thee hence, Satan: for it is written, Thou shalt worship the Lord thy God, and him only shalt thou serve. [11]Then the devil leaveth him, and, behold, angels came and ministered unto him.

The following story illustrates the power of the Word: Shanab had just been through a rough time. The last three months had been difficult. His wife Andina, whom he loved very much, just became sick. The doctors were at a loss. His son who was doing well in school, now seemed to be running into trouble with the teacher everywhere he turned, but not because of anything in particular that he had done. His boss, who always had been very pleasant, turned sour and began to make life at work almost unbearable. All this happened right after Shanab and his family decided that they were going to be more than pew-warmers at church. After the pastor preached last week, the whole family went forward to rededicate their lives to God.

As all these troubles came up one after another in the same week, Andina sat down one evening and began to consider how to deal with this situation. She and Shanab decided they were going to collect articles on the various issues which now assailed their family and share the insights they had gleaned. They prayed together. Shanab and Andina had never seem themselves as "one of those Bible thumpers." As strange as it may seem, however, they did not resolve to read the Scriptures. They read many things; they combed the pages of the Times, Ebony, Jet, Essence, Psychology Today, and other books for insight into their situation and how to deal with it. At church, they held onto every word spoken from the pulpit. One Sunday, the pastor preached from Matthew chapter 4 on how Jesus used the Word of God to fight the battles that He encountered. As the minister was speaking, Shanab turned to Andina and said, "Why don't we start studying the Bible together?" To which she replied, "I was just thinking the same thing." They both began to study Scripture more intensely. Two months later they were have a conversation and they both expressed how much insight they had gained from the Word of God. Shanab remarked about how contemporary the Word of God seemed to be. Andina shared how she had slowly been using the insights gained from the Scriptures to order her life. Shanab said, "I noticed, and I am so proud of you, and I thank God." The Word of God helped this family gain insight into the will of God for their lives.

Matthew 4:1-11—In this passage of Scripture, we read that after being baptized by John, Jesus is led into the wilderness to be "tempted by the devil." The Greek word translated "tempted" means to test one's character or virtue by enticement to sin. Jesus had to prove His allegiance to do the will of the Father. Satan wanted Him to fail like the Children of Israel failed in the wilderness. Would the Son of God succumb to the temptation of the devil? The fact that the Spirit leads Him into the wilderness suggests that victory is at hand.

We are told that Jesus had been fasting for 40 days and 40 nights. In the Bible, there are only two other individuals who are said to have fasted for the same amount of time: Moses (Exodus 34:28) and Elijah (1 King 19:8). Fasting is defined as "to deny oneself of nourishment for a defined amount of time." The purpose is to enable one to hear the instruction and direction of God more clearly, and to place the appetites of the body in check. Most of the time, if not always, fasting is associated with communing with God, such as Moses at Mount Sinai and Elijah at Mount Horeb. Matthew does not say that Jesus is praying, but it is implied by the fact that He was led by the Spirit into this period of testing.

The devil appears at the apex of Jesus' physical weakness. Verse 2 says He was "hungry." His body craved for nourishment. So the tempter challenges Jesus to turn a stone into bread to satisfy His hunger. Satan tries to get Jesus to cater to His physical cravings to use His power and authority to fulfill a physical desire. Jesus answered by quoting Deuteronomy 8:3. He, in essence, tells us that the desires of the flesh are not important, but the desires of God are. It is God's Word that takes precedence over everything else. Human beings do not subsist by obeying physical cravings, but they live through the internalization of God's Word.

Since Jesus used Scripture to combat the tempter, the tempter now decides to use Scripture out of context to cause Jesus to falter. The second temptation calls upon Jesus to test God's promise in Psalms 91:11-12. This promise ensures protection from an enemy or some mishap. The tempter suggests that Jesus should test God's promise by throwing Himself off the pinnacle of the temple to see if the angels will catch Him. Jesus replied by quoting Deuteronomy 6:16 which says that God is not to be tested.

In the third and last temptation, the tempter offers Jesus the kingdoms of the earth in exchange for Jesus' worship and allegiance. Jesus again quotes Scripture, Deuteronomy 6:13. He states that God alone should receive worship and allegiance. After this, the tempter leaves Jesus and He is ministered to by the angels. By passing these tests, Jesus shows that he is sold out to fulfill the will of God. There is no place for self-gratification, aggrandizement, or selfish greed. Jesus has become the example of the perfect servant of God. He is now able to go and call others to discipleship to follow Him as He fulfills His mission to bring glory to God and to give Himself as a living sacrifice.

What Is the Word?

The Word As A Person

In the Matthew 4:1-11, the key instrument is the Word. It should be remembered that a word in Hebrew and Greek thought was not merely sound but was the expression of the inner disposition of the speaker. Thus when the word is used, it is inclusive of the thought from which the word is born. So a person's word is really representative of the person. Because the word is the expression of the thought of the person, so what someone says really represents her or him. Within the Scripture there are, indeed, three expressions of the Word. For Christians, the Word is primarily a Person. This idea is expressed in the Gospel of John 1:1-14 where the Word of God is equated with God and, in fact, with the Person of Jesus the Messiah; Jesus as the Word of God is God. There is no Christian thought, preaching, teaching, or sharing, that is possible without this personal Word of God. In Matthew chapter 4, we encounter two modes of the Word of God. First, we encounter Jesus as the Word of God. Then we find Jesus using the Word of God, which is Scripture.

Jesus is the Word of God which communicates salvation to us. If the Word of God is a Person, then it is also relational. Jesus is the Word which relates human beings to God. All other definitions of the Word must find their grounding in Jesus as the personal Word of God spoken from eternity and history to humanity. This means that listening faithfully and acknowledging Jesus as the Word of God should be a priority for every believer. As the Word of God, Jesus is the activator of human faith. For the nature and activity to make sense to any of us, we must pay attention to Jesus as what theologians call the "Divine-Word-Event."

The Greek word "logos" that is used by John to describe Jesus as the second Person of the Trinity signifies the speech and wisdom of God. Jesus is the divine speech who arranges and orders all things. The Apostle John puts it this way, "by him all things were created, and without him nothing was made that was made" (John 1:3). When you see beauty, know that it is the Word that formed it. As the personal Word of God, Jesus embodies the excellence and the majesty of divine thought and expression.

The Word As Written

Ordinarily, when Christians refer to the Word of God they mean the Bible. In the written Word of God, God has revealed who He is in a special way. Therefore, we can actually say in the "Book of the Acts of God" because the Bible contains what God has done and will do for the world. This Book reveals God's call, God's deliverance, God's covenant relationship, God's judgment, God's restoration, and God's eternal reign. Several themes within the Bible show it to be the Word of God, but the one key theme is the theme of salvation. Throughout the Bible, we see that God is Saviour.

The Bible is not just a history book, though it speaks of historical events. In fact, we can say that Abraham, Jacob, and Isaac were historical persons. God used the Word to deliver the Children of Israel from bondage. However, the record of these historical events was written by inspiration from God. Peter puts it this way, "Knowing this first, that no prophecy of scripture is of any private interpretation. For the prophecy came not in old times by the will of man: but holy men of God spake as they were moved by the Holy Ghost" (2 Peter 1:20-21). Paul when writing to Timothy in the second letter states, "All scripture is given by the inspiration of God, and is profitable for doctrine, for reproof, for correction, for instruction in righteousness: that the man of God may be perfect, thoroughly furnished unto all good works" (2 Timothy 3:16-17). According to the scriptural records themselves, the content of this special book was inspired by God.

Anyone who desires to walk with God and have intimate knowledge of God's ways must know the Holy Scriptures. In the Scriptures, divine truths are revealed which, if we learn them, guide us truly. For the Christian, all our grounding must come from what God says to us in the Scriptures. We must not allow the Word of God to sit somewhere and gather dust, or we will be like someone who has great treasures but seldom gets to use them. As people who believe that our destiny is eternal, the Bible can guide us into a deeper understanding of what it means to have this life. The prophets and apostles did not speak from themselves, but delivered what they received from God (2 Peter 1:21). The written Word is profitable for all purposes of the Christian life. It is of use to every believer, for all need to be taught, corrected, and reproved. There is something in the Scriptures which is suitable for every situation we face. Oh, that we may love the Word more, and read them often! Then shall we find benefit, and gain the lasting happiness promised therein by faith in our Lord Jesus Christ, who is the main subject of both testaments. We best oppose error by possessing a solid knowledge of the Word of truth, and the greatest kindness we can show children is to teach them the Scriptures early.

What Can the Word Do?

In Matthew 4:1-11, we find Jesus (who is the personal Word of God) citing the written Word of God. This tells us that the Word of God serves a certain function in the lives of those who believe.

First, it serves as our defense against the attack of the enemy. Look at how many times Jesus responded to the tempter with the words, "It is written." If, as Paul says to Timothy, all Scripture is God-inspired, then the Holy Spirit is at work in the Word. When Jesus cites the written Word, He activates the power of the Holy Spirit. Many times we read in Scripture that the Word is a sword. When Jesus faced the devil in the spiritual warfare in the

Matthew chapter 4, He used the Word.

Second, the Word of God can be helpful for interpreting life's experiences. Many times in Scripture the prophets cite the Law of Moses to interpret what God was doing in their time (Ezra 3:2; Daniel 9:11-13). The New Testament is particularly full of these examples (Matthew 1:22; 2:5, 15, 17; Mark 7:10).

Third, the Word of God functions to give us a right understanding of God's nature. Scripture places a heavy premium on having a good understanding of God. A good understanding of God is important for a right worship of God. That is precisely why the Decalogue begins with "Hear O Israel, the Lord your God is One God" then proceeds to say, "Thou shall love the Lord thy God with all your heart and him alone shall thou worship" (Deuteronomy 6:4-5). In the Bible, we discover how faithful women and men have worshiped God. We also find the kinds of worship that are not acceptable to God. The Word of God functions to enlighten our soul. The psalmist was clear about this when he said, "The entrance of the word gives light" (Psalm 119:130). The Word of God helps us to act right. "Thy word have I hidden in my heart that I might not sin against thee," says the psalmist (Psalm 119:11).

Fourth, the Word functions as a corrective to our human tendency to embrace the things that wound the heart of God. Thus Paul tells us that is profitable for instruction (2 Timothy 3:16). Over and over again, we hear Jesus refer to the Scripture as a way to correct the tendency of His audience to misrepresent God and God's work in the world. (See Matthew 21:42; 22:31-32; 26:54-56; Mark 12:24.)

How Can the Word of God Become Effective in Your Life?

First, for the Word to be effective in our lives, we must know the Word of God. One way to get to know the Word of God is to read it. Jesus practiced reading the Scriptures. We know this from the way He quoted them. We are also told in Scripture that it was His custom to read the Scripture in public. If you have had the privilege of learning to read and write, there is no reason why you should not be reading the Scripture to find out what treasures God has laid in store for you in his word.

Second, we need to hear the Word of God. Many times in the Bible we read the phrase: "Hear the word of the Lord." The Bible says, "Faith cometh by hearing and hearing by the word of God" (Romans 10:17). Listening to the spoken Word of God can produce faith, (Romans 10:14). As the Word of God enters into our being, it has the power to lead us to the point of salvation (Romans 1:16). Be encouraged to make listening to the Word of God

a top priority in your life. When you hear the Word preached, ask yourself what God's Word is for you in the message instead of sitting in judgment on how well the preacher or the speaker presents the Word. We must learn to listen with humility. But this does not mean that we listen without discernment. We must listen with discernment, for whatever word we hear is the word by which we shall be judged. In the story of the rich man and Lazarus, there is a strong warning that if we do not listen to those who bring the message to us everyday, we set ourselves up for condemnation (Luke 16:19-31). The key to receiving the power inherent in the Word is found in hearing. But those who speak the Word must do so in truth. Even when you witness to the word of God, you must do so in truth (Jeremiah 23:28-29; 2 Corinthians 2:17). Because hearing the Word is so important, Jesus warns us to be careful how we hear (Mark 4:24). The Word is that seed that bears righteous fruit (Luke 8:11). It will help you cut through the morass of human mess and give you direction in confusion (Hebrews 4:12-13).

Third, we must make the Word which we have read or heard such an important part of our lives that it becomes a part of our thinking process. This is called "meditating upon the Word." Some people take the time to memorize the portions of the Scripture from which God is speaking to them. Although some people are unable to memorize Scripture word for word, it is still important to develop a way of remembering the Word of God to experience its effectiveness in your everyday life. Another way to make it a part of your life is to share findings from the Word of God with others. The formation of our thinking process by the word of God is vital for our maturity of faith. In the Hebrew testament the most frequently used word is "thought" (Hebrew *machashebheth,* from the verb *chashabh,* "to think"), which refers to the ability to have firm purpose. As Christians, our purpose must be formed by the Word of God. In the New Testament, the word *dialogismos* (Matthew 15:19; 1 Corinthians 3:20) translated as the word "dialogue" refers to the inner reasoning or deliberation that one has with oneself. Similarly, The Old Testament often translates the verb *amar,* "to say," to mean what one says to himself; and hence implies a definite and clearly formulated decision or purpose (Genesis 20:11; Numbers 24:4; Ruth 4:4). This meaning is illustrated by the change made in Esther 6:6 of the Revised Standard Version (British and American) where "thought in his heart" from the King James Version becomes "said in his heart."

Fourth, do not be afraid to apply the Word of God in your life's contexts. There is really no greater way to make God's Word part of our life than to practice it daily. When we study or listen and interact with the Word of God, it helps us to gain insight on our situation and to cope with it in realistic ways. Our spiritual health advances as we progress in the knowledge of God's Word. We can also apply it in our relationships with those around us. As we study the Word of God, we develop an inner stability which allows us to maintain our integrity through the various crises that we face in this world. Many people attempt to deal with life's stresses by getting involved in all sorts of hype. The Christian, however, has a standard source which is the Word of God. Many of our problems stem from our spiritual disequilibrium. If our problems stem from spiritual imbalance, we must find the solution in the spiritual principles inherent in the Word of God. But in do so we must be careful not to use the Word of God as an excuse for not doing the things we need to do to maintain our own health. There is a factor of realism in the Word of God which will not excuse us if we choose to ignore the simple guidelines for life which God has laid out. But when all is said and done, the Word of God is still the instrument for development toward the practice of a life of victory.

By making the Word your partner in your everyday life, you will blossom into the beautiful creature that God created you to be. The Word of God is available for you. It is your weapon for the spiritual battle you must wage in this world. It is your light for the journey which we all must travel as we pass through this vale of tears. Only by immersing ourselves in all the manifestations of the divine Word, can we keep in step with the Master, even Jesus who is the Messiah.

Chapter Three

YOU ARE INVITED

Matthew 3:1-12

In those days came John the Baptist, preaching in the wilderness of Judaea, [2]And saying, Repent ye: for the kingdom of heaven is at hand. [3]For this is he that was spoken of by the prophet Esaias, saying, The voice of one crying in the wilderness, Prepare ye the way of the Lord, make his paths straight. [4]And the same John had his raiment of camel's hair, and a leathern girdle about his loins; and his meat was locusts and wild honey. [5]Then went out to him Jerusalem, and all Judaea, and all the region round about Jordan, [6]And were baptized of him in Jordan, confessing their sins.

[7]But when he saw many of the Pharisees and Sadducees come to his baptism, he said unto them, O generation of vipers, who hath warned you to flee from the wrath to come? [8]Bring forth therefore fruits meet for repentance: [9]And think not to say within yourselves, We have Abraham to our father: for I say unto you, that God is able of these stones to raise up children unto Abraham. [10]And now also the axe is laid unto the root of the trees: therefore every tree which bringeth not forth good fruit is hewn down, and cast into the fire. [11]I indeed baptize you with water unto repentance: but he that cometh after me is mightier than I, whose shoes I am not worthy to bear: he shall baptize you with the Holy Ghost, and with fire: [12]Whose fan is in his hand, and he will throughly purge his floor, and gather his wheat into the garner; but he will burn up the chaff with unquenchable fire.

The Gospel of Matthew is unique in its focus on the Jewish people. It was probably written in Aramaic. Following the Book of Malachi, it points to the break of prophetic silence by the appearance of John the Baptist. Matthew, like the other Gospels, introduces John in his appearance in the wilderness of Judea. The motif of the desert is common to the Hebrew tradition. When Matthew begins with the motif of the dessert, he is sure that the people of Israel will understand its significance. It was in the wilderness that God trained Israel to know their God and purged them of their affection for other deities. The desert is not always an uninhabited place when used by writers of Scripture. It may just refer to open country. The importance of the desert is also seen in the fact that even Jesus is led to the desert to be tempted by the devil. When He emerges from the desert, He comes in power to do ministry. Having come from an encounter with God, John is now ready to proclaim both the holiness and grace of the God of Israel. Having spent time with God, he is able to face the leaders of Israel with courage.

In A.D. 28, John came as a prophet. According to Christian understanding, he broke a 400 year silence of prophetic utterances. Malachi had ended his prophesy with a threat that God will send "Elijah the prophet before the coming of the great and dreadful Day of the Lord. And He shall turn the heart of the fathers to the children, and the heart of the children to their fathers, lest I come and smite the earth with a curse" (Malachi 4:5-6). For Elijah was that prophet who judged Israel by the power of God and led her back to godly worship. Many Israelites were expecting the Messiah's appearance. But before this they expected someone to warn and prepare them so that they could truly turn their hearts to God's ways. They knew from Malachi that they must prepare their hearts for the Messiah's coming or they would be left out of God's great blessing.

When John came, he had a sense of urgency which reminds me of Isaiah's when he said, "Today is the day of salvation, Now is the time." With strong words, John called out to the people who came to listen to his message, "Repent, for the kingdom of heaven is near" (Matthew 3:2). John, though concerned about the future of Israel, knew that the only way they could have a future was through an immediate response to the divine invitation. There was no true future if their immediate situation of unbelief and spiritual arrogance was not healed. Instead of focusing on tradition and family piety, John focused on the state of the person and their actions. His listeners were to become personally responsible to God and to one another for their actions.

John the Baptist is not only the forerunner of Jesus, he also foreshadows Jesus. John's ministry is a microcosm of Jesus'. Both were sent by God (Matthew 11:10; 10:40); both preached repentance and the coming of the kingdom of heaven (3:2; 4:17); both of them were in conflict with the religious authorities (3:7-10; 9:3); both had disciples; and both died a violent death (14:3-12; 27:37). The differences were that John never healed anyone, nor was his death redemptive. Furthermore, Jesus never baptized, and His death and resurrection opened the door for all who trusted in Him to obtain salvation. In this chapter, we look at the invitation which God gives to the people through John the Baptist and what that means for us who are called of God today.

You Are Invited

God's invitation comes to us at different times and in different conditions. It may come to us while we sit in quietness or while we tamely contemplate the meaning of life. This invitation comes to the gentle as well as the wild. It may come in the morning, noon, night, or the time of dawn. It may come in the brightness of the day or the thick darkness of the night.

God's invitation to us may come in different places. For the people invited through the message of John the Baptist, the invitation was given in the wilderness. The wilderness was a place of lonesomeness. It, by implication, was a place of the wasted. So for those who are in hard places in their lives, for those who are in places where they are experiencing desolation caused by a world which forsakes God, this invitation comes to you. If you are solitary and feel abandoned like the people to whom John the Baptist spoke, you are invited. This invitation is open 24 hours everyday, every year. It is open in good days as well as bad days. It is an all-weather invitation. There is no weather so extreme that it can forestall this invitation. In every period, whatever the definition of your context maybe, whatever your age, and no matter what other people or even you have judged yourself to be, the invitation is for you.

How Does This Invitation Come to You?

It comes through the preaching of the Gospel. We are told that "John came preaching." The Greek word is *Kerusso* (pronounced **kay-roos'-so**). This invitation comes through heralds called by God to be public criers and proclaimers of special divine truth revealed in the Gospel. So here then John is an example of the Christian as one who is invited by God to invite others to the abundance of God revealed in the Gospel. We are invited to preach, as in witnessing and to publish abroad the present and the coming reign of God. This means that we must say what God says about the world and about God. We are properly to lay out before the world the promise of God and the dangers of rejecting the salvation offered to the world through the Lord

Jesus Christ. We are invited to relate to the world through systematic discourse or through simple conversations or through just living our lives before the world. This is how we invite the world to experience the goodness of God. While pastors may be called to speak specifically to the care of the flock of God, generally each Christian must become able to express God's offer for himself or herself. Christians in our days are still being invited to break the silence and invite their neighbors to receive the Gospel. As we have been invited, we must extend this invitation by asking, biding, and calling. We must also be able to describe and name the content of the event to which we are heralds so that those who are invited might come with a level of understanding.

The Purpose of the Invitation

When John the Baptist is introduced, he is in the wilderness of Judea, calling the people to repent. The Greek word translated "repent," means to change ones' mind for the better. The usage in this passage goes further, in that it also encompasses a change of behavior (3:8). John says that our repentance should be evident in our behavior, or "fruits." Used here, it implies a total alteration of the mind, a change in judgment, disposition, and affections. It means to become different and to give a positive bias of the soul. John is saying, "Consider your ways, change your minds; you have thought amiss; think again, and think aright." True penitents have other thoughts of God and Christ, sin and holiness, of this world and the other, than they had before responding to the call of God. The change of the mind produces a change of ways. That is the Gospel's repentance, which flows from a sight of Christ, from a sense of His love, and from hopes of pardon and forgiveness through Him. We are encouraged to repent. It is clear, John seems to say that your sins shall be pardoned upon your repentance. We are called to return to God in a way of duty, and God will, through Christ, return unto us in the way of mercy. It is still as necessary to repent and humble ourselves, to prepare the way of the Lord, as it was then. John's life shows there is a great deal to be done. To make way for Christ into the human soul is more needful than the discovery of sin. A conviction that we cannot be saved by our own righteousness is more important than our merits. His life shows that the way of sin and the world is a crooked way, but to prepare a way for Christ, the paths must be made straight (Hebrews 12:13). It also shows that those whose business it is to call others to mourn for sin, and to mortify it, ought themselves to live a serious life, a life of self-denial and contempt for the world. By giving others this example, John made way for

Christ. Many came to John's baptism, but few kept to the profession they made. There may be many forward hearers, where there are few true believers. Curiosity and love for novelty and variety may bring many to attend good preaching, and to be affected for a while, yet most are never are subject to the power of it. Those who received John's doctrine, testified to their repentance by confessing their sins. Only those who are ready to receive Jesus Christ as their righteousness, and who are brought with sorrow and shame to own their guilt receive the benefits of the reign of God. The benefits of the kingdom of heaven, now at hand, were thereupon sealed to them by baptism. John washed them with water, in token that God would cleanse them from all their iniquities, thereby intimating that by nature and practice, all were polluted, and could not be admitted among the people of God, unless washed from their sins in the fountain which God was to open (Zechariah 13:1). The Greek word *metanoeo* (**met-an-o-eh'-o**) is a combination two Greek words (*meta*) meaning beyond and (*noieo*) meaning to think. Thus we are invited to *reconsider* our moral *feeling and develop a contrite compunction.* This invitation is for us to exercise our minds in the direction of divine things. Rather than paying attention to the things which are mainly fleeting and temporal, we are called to observe, comprehend, and ensure that our minds are grasped by the things of God. Within this is the idea that if we respond to the invitation to think or reason with God, we may be led to heed and follow God's call.

The reason for repentance is that "the kingdom of heaven is near." The kingdom of heaven which John and later Jesus (4:17) preached about is not a socio-political kingdom, although it has socio-political implications. It is a spiritual kingdom based on spiritual principles, of which Jesus elaborates in chapter 5 of Matthew. John mentions that this kingdom is "near," meaning that it is imminent. It is so near that even the King himself is coming to be baptized. John identifies himself as the one who would come before the King and call the people to prepare the way. He quotes Isaiah 40:3, identifying himself as "a voice" calling a wayward Israel to repent.

We are invited simply to be a part of the reign of God. The divine order to which we are being invited is the *basileiou tou Theou* which is Greek for "the reign of God." We are invited to participate in God's new reign. But more than that, we are being invited to be, if I may say, "royalty." We are invited to rule with God. In this world, we become concrete manifestation of the divine realm or evidence of the kingdom of God. In Peter, we are told "You are a royal priesthood"(1 Peter 2:9). Paul says, "We shall also reign with him" (2 Timothy 2:12). We are being invited to become part of the heavenly reign. This is supported by the use of the word "heaven," Greek *ouranos,* (**oo-ran-os'**). As people invited by God, we are being elevated just by the idea of being invited. Being invited by God confers a status upon us. We are being invited to enter the abode of God, and it implies that we can now share in the joy of God. It also means that we now share in the power and, ultimately, in God's eternal life. We are children of the Gospel fitted for the heavenly sky.

When we are invited, we who have been afar from God, are made to draw near. The Greek word *eggizo* (**eng-id'-zo**) reflects one's willingness to approach another or the putting of something in the vicinity of another. Not only is God inviting us to come near, God has brought near to us the power necessary for realizing what God promises. The kingdom of God is near. By inviting us into the divine presence, God has made sure that we will not miss the reign of God's peace. This also means God is drawing us away from our tendency to darkness to bring us into the light of God (see John 3:18-21). But the idea that the kingdom is near is not meant to signal something placid or static, rather it is meant to convey the idea of urgency. The idea here is that of speed. What John is trying to convey here is that the kingdom of God is like a car in full throttle and in a hurry to a different destination. This invitation is not forever though its consequence is everlasting. The engine that drives this train is the Word of God as revealed in the person of Jesus Christ. It is as though God is pouring forth water and those in dry and thirsty lands are being called to bring their containers and fill them. In a sense, it can be said that God is moving toward us with outstretched arms. Those who are instrumental in inviting others to come near to God must be prophetic. This invitation should not be done in the flesh. John's invitation was inspired by the very God who commissioned him to send out the invitation.

Not only is the world being invited to come to God, but we who have responded to the invitation must show and make known God's intention to those who are being invited. This invitation, we must assure the world, comes from God's goodwill toward human beings. This invitation is to life; it is to peace; it is to comfort, and it is for the world to come and participate in the righteousness of God. With our voices and actions, we disclose the riches of God's kingdom and articulate its implication as we continually address the world on behalf of our God. This invitation must come in the language that the people to whom we are sent can understand. We ought be so careful to present the invitation in the Spirit of the God who invites, that we keep out unnecessary noises and sounds, and voices that do not reflect divine intent. As those invited to invite, we are to remain faithful in duty though the world remains prolonged in its form of ungodliness. We must shout from the by-ways and the thoroughfares. We may sometimes have to do so in a tumultuous way, crying aloud until those in the way of death hear and turn to life. We must say to the world, "You are invited."

John, as one who invited people to God, was considered mainly as one who prepared the way. He was not the way, but one who prepared the way. Those who send out the divine invitation should not confuse their power to invite with the origin of the power. As messengers of God's invitation, we are the ones who, like John the Baptist, make ready the way for the Lord. The Greek word used to describe John the Baptist's work the *hetoimazo,* (pronounced **het-oy-mad'-zo**) which means to actively prepare or provide a reason for someone to do something. Our invitation helps to make people ready to receive the Gospel. When John the Baptist says, "Prepare the way of the Lord," he is not merely saying come, he is also inviting the people to prepare themselves thoroughly. The Greek word used here, *kataskeuazo* (pronounced **kat-ask-yoo-ad'-zo**), is derived from the idea of being prepared with all the internal and external equipment necessary for battle or for travel. We are invited to a standard of internal spiritual fitness that befits the reign of our great God. Another way of looking at this is to see us as those who are invited to construct, create, build, and help make a new world with God. This invitation is awesome. We are invited to participate in God's work and to walk side by side with God. What an amazing thing!

John was inviting the people to prepare the way, Greek *hodos* (**hod-os**). The word literally means a road, but by implication it means progress. Some people think that God invites us to be stagnant. Sometimes it seems that religious people want the world to stand still. The world sometimes sees the Christian as one who fights against everything that benefits human beings. But the word here suggests that Christians are invited to orient themselves to true progress—divine progress. No one who is invited on a journey remains where they are, if they are serious. To answer the invitation of God is to be "en route" to somewhere. The invitation is for us to become pilgrims with a purpose. We are invited to stay on course and go the distance. The mode and the means for the journey on this pilgrim highway have been provided. All anyone has to do is accept the invitation.

John was inviting the people of Israel to engage their God directly. Those who answer the invitation agree to be appointed as God's emissaries. What shall anyone give to respond to an invitation to band together with the Creator of the universe? Responding to this invitation means that we are

willing to bear or bring forth fruits befitting God's invited guests. It is an invitation committed to the content of the divine process. This is an invitation to continually deal with God without any delay. We are invited to exercise our spiritual muscles toward the fulfillment of God's purpose. We are called to experience God's gift as we give over control and stretch forth our hands to hold the divine hand for the journeying. We are invited to keep faith with God. We are invited to allow God to lighten the load which weighs us down. We are invited to abandon the sinking ship of this world and board God's ship. If we are open enough to respond to God's invitation, none of the power of the world can move us. John's invitation, with its divine sanction, purges us and raises us up. This is an invitation to be secure and to show the work of God by yielding fruit. You are invited to be fruitful.

The invitation is to make the Lord's "path straight." The Greek word for path is *tribos* (**tree'-bos**). "Straight path" recalls David's statement, "he leadeth me in the path of righteousness" (Psalm 23). Jesus will later say "straight is the way." There are two paths or ways mentioned in the Bible. There is the path that leads to life that is often mentioned in the Book of Proverbs. Then there is the path of the wicked which leads to death (Proverbs 4:14). This path of the wicked is that path of those who forget God (Job 8:13). It is a crooked but wide path (Proverbs 2:15). This approach to life contrasts with the path of righteousness (Psalm 23:3; Proverbs 2:13; 2:20). However, the path which John is inviting the Israelites of his day to make straight as an alternative is the path of the Lord (Psalm 17:5; 25:4; 25:10). This path is a path of light (Job 24:13). What John is really inviting them to do is to begin living by the instruction of the Lord whom they call their God (Psalm 119:35; 119:105; Proverbs 10:17). He is calling them to engage the righteousness of God and to practice those qualities that mark them as God's people. The Greek word for path suggests hard work and something that has proven reliable over the years. They are to walk in the divinely proven path. What John is inviting them to do is literally to "level" with God. To be true to their conscience and to be so at once, without delay.

Who Can Respond to the Invitation?

In Matthew 3:5-7a, we are told that Pharisees and Sadducees came to John to hear the word from God. In this passage, we see that neither geographic location, class, nor status kept one from being invited. Anyone can respond to this invitation. This is, in fact, a preamble to what the Messiah will do (see Matthew 4:25; 22:9-10; John 5:35). Jesus Himself emphasized the idea of "whosoever." His invitation was extended to all and none were left out. This does not mean that all who respond to the invitation come with intentions to follow in spirit and truth. Neither does it mean that all who come to the banquet come with the desire to celebrate with the host. Some are like the man who came to the wedding without the wedding garment (see Matthew 22:11-12). John wanted them to know that although everyone was invited, they could not take the invitation lightly or refuse to meet the simplest demand of the host, who is their God in this case.

Why Some Refuse to Respond to the Invitation

John, in his invitation, points out some things that hinder human beings from responding to the invitation or cause them to respond wrongly to God's invitation. He points out that the Pharisees and the Sadducees had come to see him mainly out of pride, not from humility. While many came confessing their sins and repenting, others responded to the invitation with an air of superiority. Matthew tells us that when John "saw many of the Pharisees and Sadducees come to his baptism, he said unto them, "O generation of vipers, who hath warned you to flee from the wrath to come?" (Matthew 3:7) John's question "who had warned you?" implies that the Pharisees and Sadducees will not listen to anyone because as far they were concerned, they had the truth and did not need to listen to anyone who was not part of their group. Whenever they went to religious gatherings, they did not go to contribute to the process or to be affected by the principles within the religious context. They went to sit as judges over everything. They usually asked questions not to understand and see what new knowledge they could gain but to try to trap the one to whom they had come to judge. We find this very same type of interaction between these two groups and Jesus. So what John is saying here is that their response to the invitation was grounded in deceit. "Are you really serious?" is what John seems to be saying to this group of respondents. Self-deception may hinder people from responding authentically to the invitation of God. By calling them "a brood of vipers," John really accentuates the idea that they were sly pretenders who now acted as though they were sincere but did so mainly to catch someone in a mistake. This is like those who go to parties not to enjoy themselves but to see how they can criticize the host. Similarly there are people, who seemingly respond to the call of the Gospel by going to church, but who in reality are there mainly to seek out what they disagree with.

The group that John was castigating not only lacked authenticity, but they excused their lack of true response to the invitation of God by the fact that they were children of Abraham. In Matthew 3:9 John says, "And think not to say within yourselves, We have Abraham to our father: for I say unto you, that God is able of these stones to raise up children unto Abraham." They did not want to make a genuine personal commitment, but instead wanted to ride upon their connection to Abraham by blood. They were so caught up with their physical descent that they did not understand at that moment that John was calling them to respond holistically, mind, spirit, and body to the ways of God.

The fact that they confused physical connection with righteousness also led them to deceive themselves about God's judgment. "Surely, we will not be judged by God," they seem to be saying, "For we are the children of Abraham." Part of their refusal to respond to the invitation comes from the fact that they thought God's judgment would not come as John declared. They probably thought they had all the time in the world. But to their amazement, John says, "You are wrong." Because you go to church and because your father was a preacher and your mother "built" this church does not mean that God will delay judgment. Many people refuse to answer the invitation to join God's reign because they think that they have time. But John is telling us that judgment is now. Nobody has all the time in the world (Malachi 3:1-3; 4:1; Hebrews 3:1-3; 10:28-31; 12:25) It is self delusion for a person to wait until it pleases them to respond to the invitation for the "the axe is laid" (Luke 3:9; 23:31).

John saw that they could not respond positively because they did not have the fruit. Their lack of response was, indeed, a sign that they lacked fruit. People who reject the offer of the Gospel and yet argue that they know God, by their rejection show that they are not Children of God. Such must bear the consequence of the refusal to respond to God's invitation. (See Psalm 1:3; 92:13-14; Isaiah 61:3; Jeremiah 17:8; John 15:2.)

Consequence of Rejecting the Invitation

John says, "every tree that bringeth not forth good fruit is hewn down and cast into the fire" (Matthew 7:19). Those who reject this invitation or who refuse to respond according to God's own laid-down principles, are setting themselves up for God's judgment. It does not matter if they are in church or out of church. It does not matter if they were born in a Christian family or born in a pagan family; "the ax is laid at the root of every tree."

Furthermore, those who refused to respond to the invitation, which God has sent through the hand of John, risked missing out on the wonderful things which God was about to do for the people of Israel. John's message was an appetizer for the main course was to be delivered in the person of God's Son, Jesus Christ. If they refused to be baptized by John's baptism which was only the washing of the outer skin as a sign of repentance, how could they stand to be tried by the fire which comes from the hand of God? If they did not respond to John who was a humble desert dweller, they will probably miss the opportunity of seeing One who is mightier than John. They would miss the opportunity of experiencing the sanctifying power of the Holy Spirit who is an agent of the Messiah. If they cannot stand the small coals of John's Gospel, how can they stand the blazing heat of the Saviour's furnace?

Those who do not respond to the invitation of John shall find themselves being fanned away like chaff. For John, the Messiah comes as one "whose fan is in his hand" (Matthew 3:12). This a metaphor taken from the farmers who harvested wheat, after pounding to purge it of its chaff, used a hand-held fan to blow the chaff away. Those who refused this invitation missed the opportunity to be purified by the refining fire of the Holy Spirit. In ancient times, the chaff that was not blown away was burned. By using all of these metaphors, John is trying to help his listeners understand the serious consequences of declining this divine invitation.

Profits of Accepting this Invitation

As there are consequences for declining, there are also benefits for accepting this invitation. One such benefit is that those who accept this invitation will not miss the appearance of the Messiah. For only those who are ready to receive Him will understand His appearance. Another benefit for those who accept this invitation is that they become a candidate for the in-filling of the Holy Spirit. Such people will find stability in the Messiah and thus become like wheat which remains firm in the face of the fan. They will not burn because they are filled with the power of the Messiah. When judgment comes, those who have accepted this divine invitation have no need to be afraid for they have been covered by the power of one greater than John. Having passed through the fire of the Holy Spirit, they can no longer be hurt by the fire of divine or human judgment. The heart of John's invitation was for the people of his day to accept the Messiah, and through that, inherit the blessings long promised to the people of God. Will you accept the invitation to the Messiah's banquet?

Chapter Four

YOU ARE MADE WHOLE

Luke 6:6-11

*And it came to pass also on another sabbath, that he entered into the synagogue
and taught: and there was a man whose right hand was withered. 7And the scribes
and Pharisees watched him, whether he would heal on the sabbath day; that they
might find an accusation against him. 8But he knew their thoughts, and said to the
man which had the withered hand, Rise up, and stand forth in the midst. And he
arose and stood forth. 9Then said Jesus unto them, I will ask you one thing; Is it
lawful on the Sabbath days to do good, or to do evil? to save life, or to destroy it?
10And looking round about upon them all, he said unto the man, Stretch forth thy
hand. And he did so: and his hand was restored whole as the other. 11And they were
filled with madness; and communed one with another what they might do to Jesus.*

This passage of Scripture, concerning a man healed on the Sabbath, follows another passage in which Jesus is questioned about the Sabbath. The observance of the seventh day as the Sabbath, a day of rest, was strictly adhered to by the Pharisees. There was great stress applied as to what could and could not be done on the Sabbath. Oral tradition, which the Pharisees promoted, held that there were 39 principal activities or classes of work forbidden on the Sabbath. Certain activities such as "grinding" which included rubbing of wheat between one's hands was forbidden. Jesus was asked to explain His behavior for this very activity in 6:1-5. He answered by quoting Samuel 21:6 where David took bread, reserved for the priest, from the Temple, giving it to his men. The same story appears in Matthew 12:10, but in that passage Matthew says that the Pharisees asked Jesus whether it was lawful to heal on the Sabbath. Luke, on the other hand, says that they watched to see if he would heal on the Sabbath. The truth may be that while some watched, others were even more eager to question Him as a way of pushing Him to admit the act so that they could condemn Him. As is the case in the context of entrapments, both were present. This chapter of Luke deals with the motif of Sabbath. It essentially asks this question: What is the Sabbath for? It also meant to affirm the lordship of Jesus over the Sabbath "For the Son of Man is Lord of the Sabbath" (6:5). While the first five verses of the story occur outdoors, the story which forms the basis of this lesson, which incidentally also deals with the Sabbath, occurs in the house of prayer.

In the story of the withered hand, Jesus shows He has authority over life and law by healing a man on the Sabbath. The scene begins with Jesus teaching in the synagogue. He noticed a man in the crowd with a deformity. Luke tells us that the scribes and Pharisees were watching to see if Jesus would heal this man. According to their oral law, it was all right to rescue an animal from a ditch on the Sabbath, but it was unlawful to practice medicine on the Sabbath. The scribes and Pharisees were looking for an opportunity to discredit Jesus. The scribes were experts in the law. They were both theologians and jurists. They were known to serve as government officials, as teachers, and as judges, because of their knowledge of the Mosaic Law. Jesus, aware of their plot, posed a question to them. He knew they could only answer in the positive. "I ask you, which is lawful on the Sabbath: to do good or to do evil, to save life or to destroy it?" (6:9). After a moment of silence, Jesus commanded the man to stretch out his hand. When he did so, his hand was restored. The scribes and Pharisees were angry because they had been made to look foolish. Jesus had shown again that their attempts to gain righteousness by adding to the law was futile. They misunderstood the purpose of the law. Instead of using it to bring freedom and life, they used it to bring bondage by mundane rules.

Jesus Can Make Us Whole

The Scriptures are very clear that Jesus was concerned with the whole of the human being. He healed all kinds of diseases both physical and spiritual. The miracles of healing the human body were meant to affirm the fact that Jesus, as He who was in the beginning, was God's arm bringing health to persons who were sick physically and mentally. The Bible records several instances of Jesus healing people. At other times, He gave His disciples the power to carry out ministry in which healing was an important part (Matthew 10:5-10; Mark 6:7-13; Luke 9:1-6). In this case, the man was paralyzed in one hand. This man, though he was sick physically, came to the house of God to receive from God what the society could not give him. His body was sick, but his spirit may have been also. Nevertheless, notwithstanding this, he was in the presence of the Lord. The fact that this man was there is a credit to him. It may be that he still believed that God would heal him. It could be that he was determined to love the Lord in spite of his physical condition. Whatever may have been his reason, Jesus reached out to him.

Many times Jesus healed people because they asked and believed. For example, the blind man in the Gospel of John, the woman with the issue of blood who took it by faith, and the centurion's servant who was healed by the agency of his master's faith. But there were times when Jesus healed without a direct request. So the issue is not always how much faith one may have or the loudness of one's cry. For the people whom Jesus healed included those who called upon him in faith, and bystanders who probably never expected to be healed, such as the man beside the pool of Siloam. But many times Jesus healed physically in order to reach in and heal spiritually. Speaking to the woman who was hemorrhaging, Jesus said, "Thy faith hath made thee whole" (Mark 5:34; compare Matthew 9:29).

In this case of the man with a withered hand, Jesus does not ask him whether he wanted to be healed. In the case of the father of the little boy who was sick, Jesus required the father who came on behalf of his son to exercise faith for the healing of his son to which he responded "Lord, I believe, please help my unbelief" (Mark 9:23-24). But in the case of this man with the withered hand, He did not ask him for faith. The most common methods of healing Jesus used were speaking words and touching the sick person with His hand. On occasions, Jesus combined both of these. He used only words in the raising of Lazarus (John 11:43) and the healing of the ten lepers (Luke 17:14). Healing was sometimes done at a distance as in the case of the nobleman's son (John 4:50) and at the pool of Bethesda (John 5:8). (See also Luke 22:51; Mark 5:27; 5:29; 6:56; 7:33; 8:23; John 9:6-7.) Though Jesus had the power to heal, He never spoke badly about physicians. In fact, He used them as a positive image of what He came into the world to do (See Matthew 9:12; Mark 2:17; Luke 5:31). God has often healed by the ways dedicated scientists had been led into the discovery of how our human body functions. One African doctor that the writer knew when growing up used to say, "I diagnose, God heals." Here we find Jesus healing a man who may have lost hope in the possibility of his own healing or he may have made peace with his condition. Important also is that this healing takes place on the Sabbath. The Hebrew *shabbath*, the "Sabbath," means simply a day of release or day of repose from labor. It was the day in which God rested from all labor, a day declared by God to be blessed. This day was to be a blessing for all God's people. In a sense, this is a day of God's release, and this child of God was present here with an ailment. Yet here we find that the Pharisees will not allow this man to be healed on the same day which God has declared to be wholesome. They would not let him come to the Great Physician. By coming into the presence of the Master, he places himself on the path to healing. We know that to be whole we must keep in step with the Master Physician of our soul.

Who is Sick?

The underlying problem posed by this passage is this: Who is sick? Was it the man who was physically disabled or the Pharisees who were unable to appreciate the love of God and the divine healing power available for the man? There are all kinds of sicknesses in the world. Some of the sicknesses are very easy to define. Some sicknesses are even easy to heal. Others, however, defy diagnoses and prognosis. In this passage, we find a man who is physically sick. His sickness was obvious. He knew it; everyone knew it. We also find people who were sick but did not know or refused to acknowledge their need for healing. Though here we are looking at physical illness, there are various kinds of sicknesses in the world. There are sicknesses of the body and there are sicknesses of the soul. Think about the spiritual sickness of the love of money which plagues many in our day. Think about the malaise of unbridled ambition which causes us to step on one another. What about the sickness of sexual perversity. All of these, Jesus is able to heal. For, is not every sin a spiritual sickness that weighs down the soul, affects the body, and leads to both spiritual and physical death? Does not human sickness lead us to love other things with such intensity that they cloud our reverence and undo our preservation? The sickness of self-glorification is not less a problem in our time. So when we read that Jesus healed their sick, we are not merely looking at the healing of physical ailments but also at the healing of numerous sickly states that afflict humankind. Many among us are weak and sickly spiritually. Oh, how we knit a plaited band of sickness and shun our need for the Great Physician. Some of us slip into sin so easily, and we do not seem to grasp how it affects our whole being. Is it not sickness when we insist on doing that which destroys us instead of turning to the loving

God with all our soul and all our heart and our mind? Is it not sickness when we seem to love our own misery and glory in our fallen ways more than life? Our sickness affects our relationships with our spouse, our children, and our friends. Thus we can say that all of us are suffering from something worse than the weakness and sickness which affected the man in this passage. Many of us have more than a withered hand; we live a withering existence.

What about the sickness of spiritual drowsiness and sleepwalking which afflicts so many of us even in the church? How often do we who claim to be spiritually healthy, nevertheless, go sleepwalking our way through spiritual quakes? What about those of us who ought to take heed and watch and pray but prefer to slumber and ignore the voice which calls us into the light? Are we not sick? Was it just this man in this passage that was sick? The lack of attentive spiritual presence and the defiling of imagination and the setting at naught of divine authority is so common in our day. Is that not sickness? Often sickness results from living in an atmosphere which promotes vanity, encourages demonic fancies, and distorts divine blessings. What about our sickness of self-deception? So when we read in Scripture, "And He healed their sick," we must understand that this speaks of all us. For as the prophet says, "the whole head is sick" (Isaiah 1:5).

Receiving and Rejecting the Offer of Wholeness

This sick person did not implore the Great Physician with tears, though it would seem that he hoped to be healed. There was something in him that reached out to the presence of Jesus. When Jesus said, "stretch forth thine hand" something within him responded. This is what he had been waiting for all his life. Though he may not have known how to ask for it, God through the Son Jesus Christ, answered the inner desire of his soul for wholeness. Like so many sick people who came to Jesus, he must have come expecting to be made whole. But the truth is that Jesus as God knew that all of humanity was sick in the sight of God. Christ came to heal the sick. At least in the Scripture we are told that human sickness is more than physical illness. No one should think that they do not need the Great Physician. "For all have sinned, and come short of the glory of God" (Romans 3:23). Though we are all sick, there are those who have come to this Great Physician, cleaving to Him, listening to Him, respecting His prescription, following Him, and have received healing for our soul. He has received those of us who come to Him without disdain. He has healing for us who come even in the presence of Pharisees and law-mongers. He will heal us freely with his favor. He is able to cure our sin-sick soul by God's Almighty power. When He received us to Himself and named us to be His own, He became our healer. Oh how our hearts must rejoice that we have a great healer in the person of our Lord! Our Great Physician, blessed are You. Thank You Lord.

The Pharisees in this passage were another sort of sick people. They had already become infatuated with their sickness and iniquity. Worst of all, they did not know themselves to be sick. This sort of people mocked and still mock the Great Physician because He receives sick people. But such will hear the Master say, "They that be whole need not a physician, but they that are sick" (Matthew 9:12). To them he says, "Say you are well, if you must," "I am not come, to call the righteous, but sinners. . ." (v.13). If you are sick and you do not come to Him, there can be no true healing. It is for the sake of the sick and fallen that Jesus came. The Great Physician came down from heaven to prepare healing for us, not from earthly herbs and chemicals, but by His own blood. But the Pharisees, like many in our world and our churches today, were the sort of sick who could not accept and cleave to the Physician, that they might be healed. Instead of coming to the Great Physician for the healing of their sickness, they mocked the Physician, and abused the sick. I cannot help but wonder. Why were they so angry that Jesus would heal this man who needed Him so much when they themselves could have just reached out and been healed? You see, some of us today, like the people in that synagogue, instead of taking hold of the Great Physician, would also have plotted to arrest Him, bind Him in chains of our limitations, torture Him with whips of our cynicism, crown Him with thorns of most vile acts, hang Him on the cross, and paint Him with the brush of shame. Instead of seeking the manifestation of the love of God, many of us like the religious leaders in this passage, choose to concentrate on rules and regulations without spiritual power. We barricade ourselves with details that have very little to do with the work of the kingdom of God. Like the leaders we are sometimes threatened by anyone who wishes to break others loose from the little spiritual, stereotypical cells into which we have put them. We tend to hide our sickness by concentrating on form without spiritual fervor, and on course outlines without content. We create a new Babel, and a meaningless cacophony of cliches which we hope will hide the fact that we are in need of the Balm of Gilead. When our little world of rules and regulation is threatened, we turn quickly to the weaponry of words. But while we use words as fig leaves for our nakedness, Jesus, the Master Physician uses them as signs that leads us to health. He speaks the word and it makes us whole.

Another interesting fact here is how some of us, like our brothers in this text, seem to think that human sickness can be subverted by inventing meaningless ritualism. But Jesus comes in with no fanfare, with no class of priest to burn His incense; He merely speaks the word of healing. Now that is what makes sick people, who would rather remain sick and wish that others would feel exactly like them, become extremely mad.

Being Made Whole

How can we be made whole? First, we must not forget the Cross or the character of our Lord if we are to be made whole. Whether our sickness has physical or spiritual symptoms, the Lord manifests patience to us, and pours out healing love. Our pain may be raging all over us. We may have known disease and depression, yet now we see with our inner eyes the Physician who came to offer us divine healing. If our sickness is hatred, hear the Great Physician as He speaks a word of life on behalf of the those infatuated with death: "Father, forgive them; for they know not what they do." Let His healing power make you whole. If your sickness is malignant cruelty, which is always seeking a fight even with those who seek to help you, hear the healing waters of His love as He says, "Greater love has no man than this that a man lay down his life for his friends." You need to know that He sees all your sickness and pain. He knows the pain caused to by others. Jesus offers you and yours, yes all of us, wholeness. But first you must come into His presence. Second, you must not try to hide your plight. He already knows them. It will be foolhardy to try to act as if He, being God, does not know that you are sick.

As He stood in the midst of the synagogue and healed the man for whom the religious leaders did not seem to care, He stands willing and waiting to heal you. He healed this man by speaking. The sick must hear His voice and listen. Oh my, how some sick people can be mean, yet how meek and compassionate the Lord is in offering healing even to the mean. The leaders of Jesus' day despised and delivered Him to death. Yet even in their hate, His healing did not stop as He said, "Father, forgive them, for they know not what they do" (Luke 23:34). His voice of healing continues to speak. It will not be in vain. O, that you will reach out and touch Him and be healed! We can go further and speak of His death by which He overcame our worst malady, the fear of death. Jesus, being God, died to exchange our sickness for health. He came to exchange our death for life. In His dying, He offers healing for our pain; in His burial, He covers our shame and heals our guilt. In His rising again, He restores us to divine health. In ascending, He has placed

us in the center of God's healing heart. We are in heavenly places with Him. That healing did not stop. For He sent the Holy Ghost to us who wait patiently for the promise of healing. He sent the Holy Spirit to heal our stammering tongue and break down our spiritual walls. He has become present with us that we might unlearn our hurts and replace divine wisdom for our ignorance. Within the words, "Father, forgive them, for they know not what they do," I often read, "Father, heal me for I am among the sick." The Master walks with me that I might be healed.

Accept His Sabbath of wholeness which He offers to you. In the Hebrew Testament, God promised a "Shabbath" for all who put their trust in the Lord. It is the Lord's intention to vindicate all God's children by losing us from bondage. Jesus does this by calling us to salvation or wholeness. It is not surprising that Jesus used the Sabbath, in many occasions, as a day to express the healing power of God. He did this in the case of the woman whom He healed. He healed her, but not before He expressed His displeasure with those who used the Sabbath to keep people in bondage:

> "Ye hypocrites, doth not each one of you on the Sabbath-days loose his ox or his ass, and lead him away to watering? And ought not this woman, being a daughter of Abraham, whom Satan hath bound these eighteen years, be loosed from this bond on the Sabbath-days?" (Luke 13:15-17)

On another occasion, the Lord healed a sick man by the pool of Siloam on the Sabbath and asked him to carry his mat as testimony to his healing (John 9:11-14). The religious leaders also complained. But this again confirmed that in Jesus, the Shabbath of the Lord God of Israel had come. This Shabbath was declared in Isaiah, chapter 61. The Sabbath is the declaration of the Lord's release for all those who are bound. It is the opening of prison doors; it is the opening of the eyes of the blind; it is the binding of the broken-hearted.

When the Master loosens us from our grave clothes and breathes life into our soul, even on the Sabbath, it is not contrary to the law. He healed on the Sabbath, not to break the law, but to fulfill it. The law dealing with the Sabbath is not so much a prohibition as it is a promise of peace and rest. It is a promise that we will experience the peace and victory which God experienced at the completion of creation. The Sabbath really then is time of healing. The Pharisees who did not want Jesus to heal on the Sabbath seemed to forget that the law did not prohibit men from being healed upon the Sabbaths. The priests worked to bring people into covenant with the Lord on Sabbaths. The power of the Sabbath is shown in the fact that even God allowed the rescuing of animals on the Sabbath. It is quite possible that many people came to Jesus on the Sabbath because the common theology of the day rightly saw the Sabbath as a day of healing. It was a day which the Lord has made.

God's Sabbath is meant to release us from activities that defile us. It is also meant to release us from the spirit of materialism to which many of us so easily fall prey. It is intended to temper our incessant grasping for wealth, to curtail our tendency to be busy with worldly business and so easily forget the things of God, and to make us become attentive to the spiritual exercises which contribute to our wholeness. When Jesus healed, He meant to call the people of God to a consistent reflection upon the goodness of God. Jesus offers all of us an entrance into the rest and the release of God. In this Sabbath, He voids the bills which bind our souls. He has come to offer us the Sabbath of God's wholeness. Ultimately, by His suffering death, He had made sure that we who have been exiled from God by our inner sickness might go forth in peace and without condemnation. He has healed us that we might return and find rest without fear.

Jesus, our Great Physician, has come. He offers us God's Sabbath of wholeness. Let us pray earnestly that this wholeness may come to our families, our streets, our cities, our nation, and our world. We need healing, but let us rely on God's healing balm offered in the life of Jesus. Oh, that we would live as in His Sabbath of wholeness! When we fall in this life, when we are sick, may we come into His presence as the man with the withered hand came. When He says, "Stretch forth thine hand," let us not hesitate, for He will not disappoint us. May the Lord, increase our faith. The Great Physician will not disregard us and leave us to our misery. He will lift us up and raise us to wholeness. But we must trust the word of health spoken to us by the power of God's Son. We do not have the power to heal ourselves but the Lord does. How able the Lord is! Jesus invites us, to experience His deliverance. God intends to fill us with all good things. Let us enter the rest of God's Sabbath and be made whole.

Chapter Five

YOU HAVE THE AUTHORITY

Luke 10:1-5

After these things the Lord appointed other seventy also, and sent them two and
two before his face into every city and place, whither he himself would come.
2Therefore said he unto them, The harvest truly is great, but the laborers are few:
pray ye therefore the Lord of the harvest, that he would send forth laborers into his
harvest. 3Go your ways: behold, I send you forth as lambs among wolves. 4Carry nei-
ther purse, nor scrip, nor shoes: and salute no man by the way. 5And into whatso-
ever house ye enter, first say, Peace be to this house.

Luke 10:17-20

And the seventy returned again with joy, saying, Lord, even the devils are sub-
ject unto us through thy name. 18And he said unto them, I beheld Satan as light-
ning fall from heaven. 19Behold, I give unto you power to tread on serpents and
scorpions, and over all the power of the enemy: and nothing shall by any means
hurt you. 20Notwithstanding in this rejoice not, that the spirits are subject unto you;
but rather rejoice, because your names are written in heaven.

In Luke 10, Jesus summons 70 of His disciples and gives them "authority" to cast out unclean spirits and to heal every kind of sickness. Jesus gave them authority over the evil spirits and diseases. The disciples are being sent out with the authority of Jesus. They are going out to mimic the ministry of Jesus to Israel. They will do what they have been watching Jesus do. And according to Matthew 10:7, they will also preach that "the kingdom of heaven is near," echoing John the Baptist and Jesus. In fact, it is to be their initiation into the work for the reign of God. The report of the 70 appears almost parallel in Matthew and Luke (see Matthew 9:35-10:16). It also appears in Mark 6:7-11 but not in as much detail as it does in the other two. Here Luke has just finished narrating Jesus' encounter with different kinds of would-be disciples, followers whose motives were as varied as they come. It seemed that Jesus had just established the criteria for being a true disciple of Jesus. Here He sends out those whom He believes now understand what it means to be a disciple. The sending of the 70 is significant for many reasons. It affirms the connection of Jesus with Moses who appointed 70 elders to help lead the people under the guidance of his African father-in-law. We are told that Jesus sent them because their need became too great for one person to meet. Some say that He was about to make an entrance into the Judean vicinity. Until now His ministry had been in Galilee. More importantly, Jesus is about to help His disciples understand the power that God has placed within them and the meaning of His presence in the world.

The other Gospels focus on 12 disciples. But Luke introduces us to a larger corps of close followers. Luke 10 tells us that Jesus appointed 72 that He sent out two-by-two to preach in Israelite towns. We know the names of the twelve. But the 72 remain anonymous. Yet Jesus knew them and their ministries well. How good that today too we need not be well known by others to be effective disciples of Jesus Christ. Two things should be noted: (1) Discipleship involves more than just sitting and learning. Eventually one must practice what one is being taught. (2) The mission the disciples were on was a microcosm of the mission they would continue after Pentecost. They were being prepared to turn the world upside down and spread the Gospel throughout it.

The Sending

In Luke 10, we are told of more disciples than the twelve. Jesus calls them together and gives them authority over evil spirits and power to heal every disease and sickness. The disciples are about to be sent out to the House of Israel to exemplify the ministry of Jesus. They will preach the kingdom of heaven. Their message will be accompanied by authority to perform miracles just as in the case of the ministry of the Master. Their mission is to take the Good News of the kingdom with signs that authenticate their message to the nation of Israel to bring them to a decision to follow Christ, or to reject Him. As Jesus called the twelve disciples to follow Him, He is now using the twelve to call Israel to a decision.

The disciples are given authority as Jesus exercised authority to heal and expel demonic spirits. They are to do what their Master has shown them. They are to challenge the nation to respond in faith to Jesus as He did. The word "to send" is the Greek word *apostole* which has the meaning to send with the authority of the sender. The disciples will later be labeled "apostles" meaning the "sent ones." There is a common thread that runs through both the calling and the sending, *obedience* and *authority.* In the call, there is the obedience to follow in spite of the cost. The same is true in the sending. The disciples are sent out and told exactly what to say and do. The disciples are told not to worry about their physical needs; God will supply them. Jesus also delineates the proper response to those who reject the message and says that it will be better for those in Sodom and Gomorrah than for those who reject this message.

This reminds us that the Gospel is not just for those we find socially acceptable but for all who would answer the call regardless of their situation in life. Chapter 10 illustrates our role in the spreading of the Gospel. We are the sent ones who venture out into the highways and by-ways, to the high-rises and the projects, and to the farmers and the corporate world to bring a global population to a decision. They will either answer the call in faithful obedience just like the disciples or they will reject it. Our first mission may be to our friends and associates, but from there we must branch out into the world.

The key in unleashing the power for those who are sent is obedience to voice of the Lord who sends. We must understand that we are critical to the accomplishment of the task of the kingdom. When we first decided to accept Jesus, the Son of God, as our Saviour, we became candidates for experiencing His power. If we have chosen to follow him wherever he leads and become completely dedicated to His ways, then we must be ready to take on the task of spreading the Gospel of the kingdom of God. True discipleship does not ignore that intimate relationship with the Lord, neither does it disregard the need of the community for that which it offers. Here the discipleship to which these 70 where called leads them to go beyond themselves to the community. To be effective as ambassadors of Jesus, these 70 must show His characteristics and emulate his lifestyle. They must be willing to go even to places where they had never been and to people they may not like (Luke 9:1-10). For these disciples to go, they must now trust the presence of Jesus even though he was not there with them physically. They must be ready to suffer in humility knowing that their experience is for the divine purpose. The people who are sent are ones who have come to understand the meaning of commitment. They have watched Jesus' prayer life; they have been involved with Him intimately, yet now they must show the world. The primary activity for which Jesus calls us is to lift Him up so that our world may see Him. He appoints us as those who accompany Him amidst the world. Our view of the world has been modified by seeing our Lord in His various encounters with the world, and because of our association with Him, we are now ready to be sent. Like the disciples of Jesus in the past, we now bear witness to that with which are joined. To be appointed as His disciples means that we now serve as those who mediate Christ's principles in the world. In other words, we have become, as the preachers say, "people who stand in the gap." His disciples know the intimate desire of the Saviour's heart so they are now qualified to bear His message. But their qualification is not in them, but in the One whom they have to know. Often people try to go, who have not been sent by the Lord or whose spiritual composition is not substantially connected to the Lord. But these disciples were led intimately to participate with the Master. Not only have they been in close proximity to the Saviour, His Spirit and theirs has become coextensive. He has penetrated their inner being so that they can say to those whom they meet, "We know of whom we speak." To say that the Lord appointed them is to say that these were those through whom the Lord sought to exhibit his power and authority. In Luke 10:1, when he appointed and sent them He did so *pro prosopon* "before his face." The Lord sent His own not outside of His presence but in front where His presence can protect them. This is Jesus who said "I will not leave you as orphans " (John 14:18, NIV). His appearance was going to keep away all the enemies who sought to destroy or to derail the purpose for which the disciples were called. His countenance and His presence will keep them as they went forward. This meant that their appearance would carry with it the divine approval. We also note that He sent them everywhere He intended to go. The use of the Greek word *topos* suggests that Jesus meant to send them not just to major cities but to locations of limited occupancy. They were to go to people of every condition giving everyone the opportunity to experience Jesus' offer of salvation. Where He sent them, He Himself is willing to go. He will personally supply the active principle without which they do not otherwise have the power to represent Him. He will accompany them as they go. At the precise time when they need Him, He will appear bringing with Him support from heaven. His Spirit will help them grow. His sun will light their path in the night. He will stand next to them when they are accused as many will be in the future. When tested, He will help them overcome. They know as they go that they can resort to Him whenever they needed Him. He sent them where He Himself is going.

The Meaning of Authority

When the word "authority" is used in reference to God, it means absolute power and freedom to do whatever the Lord chooses. In the Scriptures, God is seen as the source of all authority and power. The "authority" of God refers to the divine essence as author of existence. God's ability to authorize an action and a birth is articulated by the reference to God as Creator. The New Testament word translated "authority" is the Greek *exousia,* a word for which there is no exact correspondence in Hebrew or Aramaic. The Greek *exousia* expresses both freedom and legal rights, and is used in the Bible in numerous ways. When Jesus sent the disciples in this chapter, His act of sending them and their act of obedience in going out caused the power of the Spirit of Christ became active in their lives. Whatever power the sent receive, it must be understood that it is grounded in the authority which is intrinsic to the power of God (Romans 13:1, RSV; see also John 19:11). There is a sense in which the word translated "authority" from the Greek implies the act of freeing someone to act in a certain way. So here it signifies that Jesus the Son of God, in a way, is sharing the power and authority He received from God with these disciples (Matthew 28:18; John 10:18; John 17:2), enabling Him to forgive sin (Mark 2:10), and signifying His power to heal and to expel demons, which He gave His disciples (Mark 3:15). Third, it describes the freedom God gives His people for salvation (John 1:12) and from legalism (1 Corinthians 6:12). Fourth, it denotes the authority God imparted to the leaders to build up the church (2 Corinthians 10:8; 13:10). Fifth, *exousia* signifies the power God displayed through agents of destruction in the last days (Revelation 6:8; 9:3; 9:10; 9:19; 14:18; 16:9; 18:1). Sixth, the word denotes the dominion God allows Satan to exercise (Acts 26:18; Ephesians 2:2). Seventh, it describes the "authorities" created by God, both heavenly (Colossians 1:16) and secular (Romans 13:1; Titus 3:1). The term *exousia* which appears in Luke chapter 10 denotes an authority manifested in power. In fact, in some versions of the Bible such as the King James Version, the words "authority" and "power" are used interchangeably (Matthew 9:6; 9:8; 10:1; 28:18).

You Have the Authority to Harvest

We are harvesters in the vineyard of God. Jesus uses the metaphor of the harvest (Matthew 9:37-38; John 4:35-38) to describe the idea of bringing people into the reign of God. We are co-workers with Jesus in the kingdom of God (1 Corinthians 3:6-9). We cannot sit still and watch the ripened harvest go to waste. We must gather into the barn. We are the laborers with the Lord. Jesus Himself tells them that the reason for sending them is because the laborers in this harvest field are few. God has even given us authority to labor in the vineyard of God (Matthew 20:1; Mark 13:34; 2 Corinthians 6:1). It is a work for which we must be ready to sacrifice even our lives (Philippians 2:30). The ability to work in the kingdom is derived from the working of the Lord in our soul (Colossians 1:29; 4:12). Jesus appoints them to see; He intends for them know the state of the harvest. In this also He gives them the power of sight. "For the harvest is plentiful" (RSV) is an eye-opening statement from the Lord Jesus to us. It a statement which makes us understand. It is important to note that here He does not encourage to us sow the seed. He does not even tell us to water. He does not say there are too many weeds in the vineyard. All these things are important. But here Jesus concentrates on the harvest. Instead He says, "The harvest is plentiful." We must come to terms with the fact that there are many who search for the Saviour and thus are led into the trap laid out by false messiahs. For the first time, when the disciples hear that the harvest is ripe, their eyes were opened to the fact that God has been sowing seeds of righteousness into human lives since the day of Adam. Now in the fullness of time, the Son of God has ripened them. The coming of our Saviour into the world has now given the world the boost it needs to become ready for the entrance into the reign of God. The second part of this revelation is "but the laborers are few." Another key element that is involved in this process is prayer.

You Have the Authority to Pray: "Pray the Lord of the Harvest"

Jesus, in this conversation, seems to confer the special task of praying to His disciples (2 Thessalonians 3:1). Not only is God making us co-workers in the vineyard, but we are also called to seek out other laborers in the vineyard. The way of discipleship demands that we reproduce ourselves in the kingdom. But the fact is that we have the power to call people into the harvest field. The harvest field belongs to God and only God has the right to bring anyone to work there. So when you get tired of being the only one who teaches Sunday school, or the only one who ushers, or the only one who goes to do evangelism, or the only one visiting the sick, pray. The authority which Jesus confers upon His disciples to pray is more than just a notion. It the principle for the increase of the kingdom. It is amazing that God wants us to ask for help to do the work of God. If there ever was anyone who could do the work alone, it should have been the Lord Jesus Christ.

But even He sought and prayed for co-workers to do the work. Here He tells us there is no need for you to be the only one laboring in the vineyard. Your first task as teacher or preacher of the Gospel is pray for the more workers and to work to make sure that they are ready. Thus, the power to pray is a power which Jesus confers upon us in order that we may be able to practice ministry to the utmost. Through prayer, we can effectively silence the power of the enemy and help open the hearts of those who need to be part of the work of the kingdom. The idea that we should "pray the Lord of the harvest" is grounded in the fact that we are in relationship with our Lord. It must be understood that prayer is the fundamental act which prepares the ground for abundance. To be effective in winning the world for the reign of God, we must call upon the Lord (Luke 9:1; Numbers 11:17, 29; Psalm 68:11; Jeremiah 3:15; Mark 16:15, 20; Acts 8:4; 11:19; 13:2, 4; 20:28; 22:21; 26:15-18; 1 Corinthians 12:28; Ephesians 4:7-12; 1 Timothy 1:12-14; Hebrews 3:6; Revelation 2:1). Prayer is the source of our power and is the key that opens up the gate of authority to the believer. It is for this reason that Jesus said, "If you ask anything in my name it shall be done for you" (John 15:7, paraphrased).

God never denies the prayer of those who desire the coming the kingdom of truth. This authority to pray speaks to the efficacy of the believer. Through this power, the believer is indeed able to help free the world by the power of Jesus Christ. What we have received from Christ in this command to pray is the operative principle that unleashes the creative power of the Creator into our world. By this power, we can pour holy water to quench the fires of unbridled lust which plagues our lives. By the power of prayer, we become delegates of divine grace. Not only do we have the authority to pray to the Lord of the harvest to send workers, we have the power of prayer to pray as we work in the harvest. Prayer has the capacity to amplify grace and increase faith. Through it, we obtain an understanding of God's heart and depth of divine compassion.

When we take this authority to pray seriously, we come to a place where our prayer is used to push back plagues, to scatter the foes of the kingdom, to unlock showers of blessings to the needy and to turn back God's anger. Prayer alone destroys the enmity between us and God. By it we render powerless the operations of evil. By this authority to pray, the Master has conferred on us power to act in concert with God for the cause of the kingdom of God. Through the power of prayer, we recall the lost souls and cause our wandering brothers and sisters to depart from the very path of death. Through it, we help to transform ourselves, as well as other Christians, from weakness to strength. Through prayer, we call in divine restoration to the sick, we cast out spiritual wickedness which has possessed the souls of God's creatures. Is there a bar of iron? The power of prayer, will pry open prison bars of iron. Is there a chain which binds the soul? Jesus has given us the power of prayer to loose the bonds by which the enemies of our spiritual freedom have bound us. Through prayer, we are able to overcome temptations. Through it, we are able to help those who are called into the vineyard to overcome persecutions. Through our prayers, we send strength to the weak, speak joy to the down-spirited, and place a pavilion over the wearied desert pilgrim. Prayer is the key to the harvest. It is our power against the spiritual enemy who roams around like roaring lion seeking whom he may devour. Pray with all prayer, pray by day, pray by night. Paul's admonished us to "Pray without ceasing." "Pray" says the Master, "the Lord of the harvest, that he will send forth laborers into his harvest." You have the authority to pray.

You Have the Authority to Speak Peace: "In Whatever House Ye Enter, say, Peace . . ."

Jesus is the Prince of Peace. He is the Master of peace who bestows peace upon the believer. Our Master, in all that He did, taught His disciples the meaning of peace. Walking with Him they came to know the blessing of peace which flows from the heart of God. They saw what it was like to be deeply moved and yet have inner tranquility. They understood what it meant to be critical of the corruption and opulence of the day, how to experience the deep pain of the poor who had nothing going for them in this world, and yet have peace. Here was One whose love was thrown back to Him with insults, yet He remained a man of inner tranquility. It was not so much the expressive anger of the Lord that made people angry but the fact that they could not seem to touch His inner calmness. Peace does not mean inactivity. It does not mean not being angry. It does not mean inaction. It does not even mean an absence hostility. One can actually say that peace means being in the will of the God. Here, Jesus says to his disciples, "And into whatsoever house you enter, first say, Peace." The disciples were to look for those who will do the will of the Lord. This peace is connected to a willing and obedient heart.

But much more than speaking peace to another, this passage charges the followers of Jesus to be people of peace. We are to have inner peace as well as be at peace among ourselves and all peoples. They must speak peace if they are to inherit the reign of God. They are to be people of peace if they are to be effective witnesses of the peace of God. They could not be children of God if they could not speak peace. For Jesus had already told them, "Blessed are the peacemakers, for they shall be called the sons of God" (Matthew 5:9, RSV). Here was their chance to show that they indeed did believe in Him. But you know that even those who claim to worship God have often been the ones who have pursued war and strife. In fact, in the name of the Lord some have even killed their so-called enemies. To look at our world today, you would think that there has never been a message of peace. Jesus sent His disciples into a world where from every corner of the earth, and in every family, there was strife. The Romans were striving with the Jews, the Greeks with the Romans. All these people felt that this striving with one another was necessary. Yet, Jesus said "speak Peace." As for us, we live in world where believers and non-believers seem to be willing to get into conflict "at the drop of a hat." Yet we, who claim to follow the path of peace, have been called to and given the power to speak peace. But this speech of peace must come from an inner awareness of the Prince of Peace. Our Master sends us forth to preach "peace" to every house.

We say peace because we have peace. We have the power to speak peace because we know the source of all peace. For the giver of peace has given us, as Scripture says, "a peace that passeth all understanding" (Philippians 4:7). We cannot know true inner tranquility which is the reconciliation of our alienated selves with God without knowing God. Our spiritual harmony comes only fro the fact that God is with us. We have been lifted to heavenly places, where in the presence of the Lord, there is unbroken peace. Because of the sin of Adam, we were thrown to inner turmoil and outer strife. However, we who now belong to Christ have reentered the inner recesses of the Creator's heart. Thus we have obtained peace beyond even our own comprehension. The one who knows the Lord does not need to wait for eternity to know that peace which is of God. For having seen the revelation of the grace of God in the face of Jesus the Messiah, we have entered into the peace of the everlasting God. You have received peace from God so that you may speak peace to the world. God dwells in you. You have been brought into covenant with the Lord. You have the authority to speak peace to every house that you enter.

I had just become acquainted with this passage from Luke and Psalm 91:19, "Behold, I give unto you power to tread on serpents and scorpions, and over all the power of the enemy: and nothing shall by any means hurt you" concerning authority over the powers of the devil. I hated snakes with a passion. I was working on a farm with my mother when I saw a Black

Mamba. It raised its head and hissed at me. Without thinking, I just said, "Die in the name of the most high." To my amazement, the serpent slumped and died. My mother, who has now gone to be with the Lord, just looked at me calmly as if she expected it. I looked at her; goose bumps filled my body, and shivers ran down my spine. On that day, I learned the meaning of the authority which the Lord promises to those who believe.

There are many enemies which those who are sent must face as they seek to declare the glory of their Master. The old serpent with whom we war still seeks to bruise the heel of humanity; we still seek the power to bruise his head. But when we are sent by the Lord, many powers will try to impede our steps. But even He, who came in human form, has already said to us, "Thou shalt tread upon scorpions . . . and nothing shall by any means hurt you." Whatever evil that enemy sets up against human beings shall not overcome us. Evil has lost its sting; death has been deprived of its power. We have received power to rebuke the lion, even the devil, and he flees from us. Yes, his evil may be rampant against humankind in our day, but by the power of Him who sent us, we shall trample down their high places and fill their ditches. With the fire and the holy smoke of the Spirit of Christ, we shall chase them from their hiding place. In the name of the One who has sent us, we shall bind the old dragon and its vipers. For he has been made subject to the power of the resurrection. The enemy has been conquered so that even the weakest believer can tread down his high places and lead captives from the kingdom of the shadows to the kingdom of the divine light. Though the first Adam left us powerless and defeated, this second Adam, named Jesus the Christ has now conquered and made us victorious. By sending us out in His name, the Lord has made us "more than conquerors." Where the enemy brought death, in the name of Jesus, the Son of God, we come to declare life new life. Where hurt and pain and war and worry have taken possession of men, we come to declare the power of the Lord. We blow the trumpet in the hill of Zion, the power belongs to the Lord. We have been sent to declare liberation for all whom we meet. When, therefore, the Lord sends, He makes alive by imparting His very own power and authority.

What does it mean that the Lord called, appointed, and sent us out in His name? He called us to pardon us with His own righteousness. Jesus has commanded the Spirit of God to rest upon all who go out into the world in obedience to His voice. Having now become clothed with Jesus Himself as our protection, we are not afraid of being swallowed up by immorality or other corruption. He sends us out without the Holy Spirit so that darkness cannot overcome us because it cannot overcome Him who was in the beginning. The same King of Glory who calls us to follow Him and invites us to the divine banquet in honor also grants us the power of salvation. God, the Son confers eternal light and authority upon those who call on the Lord's name. Just as He had the power from God, the Father to fulfill His prophetic mission, He indeed through His infinite kindness, has shared this power with us though are unworthy. We now possess God's power because God in divine majesty has possessed our souls. We now know that we must obey the Lord who sends us, not as though we are compelled by God, but willingly. Having this power, now we are able to cancel the power of demonic oppression. The Master has placed this power in us so that those of us who yield in obedience to God's will might dispossess the principalities and indeed by God's power beome a covering for the weak. Those who have not yielded will find that they are not in possession of that goodness and power which unfetters the world. Oh, the kindness of the Master to kindly bestow on us who believe this goodness and power. We must then keep ourselves in His will and hold precious this treasury of power which has been poured into us.

In sending the disciples, Jesus knew that one of the greatest fears of the people of the ancient world was the fear of evil spirits. In this chapter, Jesus sends His disciples, and they come back to Him attesting to the fact that they were no longer afraid of the demonic powers of the world. In fact, the powers of this world were now subject to them. Fear keeps us from achieving God's divine purpose for us. If you are kept under the power of bondage in anyway, you should know that you are powerful through divine action. Your actions are now empowered by the incomparable Christ. Now that you have the power of the Lord, you can do all things. You ought not to have the fear that grips the world. You ought not to fear the devil. Having being named and sent by the Lord, you have dominion over all the devices of the devil. Jesus told His disciples that He saw "Satan fall like lightning from heaven" (Luke 10:18). There is no power of the enemy of our soul that ought to become an object of your fear. You have received power from One who is truly powerful. This power comes from One who is supreme.

The disciples who were sent understood their power as soon as they encountered the world. Not only does this power give us victory over the fear of the enemy, but imparts into our soul the discipline of Jesus. This power seals and sets us apart from the world. This power in us is the Spirit of Jesus which is God. Because we have this power, we do not converse with the works of the night. By this power, we can cast out demons. Though we may have these spiritual powers, we must hear the Lord as He instructs His disciples: "Rejoice not that the spirits are subject unto you; but rather rejoice, because your names are written in heaven." Both the casting out of evil and having one's name written in the book is done by God's power. None of these happen because of our goodness or our spiritual diligence. The Master has given us power over all the powers of the enemy. This mission is not impossible for those who are sent to perform miracles by the power of God's will.

Chapter Six

JESUS WILL COME FOR YOU

2 Peter 3:1-9

This second epistle, beloved, I now write unto you; in both which I stir up your pure minds by way of remembrance: [2]That ye may be mindful of the words which were spoken before by the holy prophets, and of the commandment of us the apostles of the Lord and Saviour: [3]Knowing this first, that there shall come in the last days scoffers, walking after their own lusts, [4]And saying, Where is the promise of his coming? for since the fathers fell asleep, all things continue as they were from the beginning of the creation. [5]For this they willingly are ignorant of, that by the word of God the heavens were of old, and the earth standing out of the water and in the water: [6]Whereby the world that then was, being overflowed with water, perished: [7]But the heavens and the earth, which are now, by the same word are kept in store, reserved unto fire against the day of judgment and perdition of ungodly men.

[8]But, beloved, be not ignorant of this one thing, that one day is with the Lord as a thousand years, and a thousand years as one day. [9]The Lord is not slack concerning his promise, as some men count slackness; but is longsuffering to us-ward, not willing that any should perish, but that all should come to repentance.

Tradition holds that 1 and 2 Peter were written by the Apostle Peter, possibly from Rome. Peter, himself, figures as a prominent disciple in the Gospels; he is generally named first among the disciples when their names are listed (Matthew 10:2; Luke 9:28; Mark 3:16). In the Book of Acts, two apostles take center stage: Peter (Acts 1-12) and Paul (Acts 13-28). Peter is also believed to be the source behind Mark's Gospel.

The Epistle of 2 Peter is Peter's letter to the church to help fight false doctrine. Jesus had promised that he would return (John 14:3, 18, 28; Acts 1:11). Yet, by the time this letter is written (approximately 64 A.D.), almost 30 years would have passed. During this period, there were false teachers preaching that either Jesus would not return or that He had already come and gone. The Apostle Paul deals with the belief that Christ has already come and gone in 2 Thessalonians 2:2ff. He assures believers that this has not happened yet, and explains what must take place before Jesus returns. Second Peter 3:1-9 deals with the false teaching that Jesus will not return.

In the first two verses, Peter wants to bring to remembrance what had been spoken before by the prophets (Isaiah 13:6; Jeremiah 46:10; Joel 3:14; Malachi 4:5), the apostles (1 Thessalonians 4ff), and the Lord (Matthew 24ff). He mentions that people were mocking in unbelief, and questioning the return of Christ. The scoffers say that nothing has changed "since the fathers fell asleep," referring to the Patriarchs, and from the beginning of creation. Their conclusion was that nothing was going to happen. But Peter reminds his readers that something has happened since the beginning of creation: the flood. As promised, God brought judgment on the earth once before by water. Verse 7 tells us that God has also reserved the heavens and earth for judgement by fire. The implication is that as God kept the first promise to destroy the earth. This promise also will be kept. Peter ascribes the delay to two things. (1) Our understanding or concept of time is different from the Lord's. God is not bound by 24 hours a day, 365 days a year. The Lord stands outside of time. (2) The Lord is patient. God is allowing time for people to repent. But God will keep His promise!

The Promise

Peter speaks of that which was promised by the prophets, and the Lord through the apostles. We will divide this section into three categories: the prophets, the Gospels (what Jesus said), and the apostles (Acts and any epistles). The promise Peter is referring to would be the Second Coming of Jesus or the Day of the Lord. The Greek word used for the appearing of Christ is *parousia* (**par-roo-see-a**).

The Prophets

The Old Testament prophets foretold of a great day of destruction which would fall upon humankind. The prophet Isaiah in 13:6-22, mentions the sun and the stars not giving their light any more, women and children being killed, and judgment falling upon the whole world because of its wickedness. But within this prophecy of doom there was always a prophecy of hope to those who trusted in the Lord God.

Jeremiah also prophesied against the gentile nations speaking of a day of vengeance, the Day of the Lord (Jeremiah 46:10-26). He speaks of a sword saturated with blood and the destruction of many nations. Joel speaks of the sun and the moon being darkened, and the stars failing to shine (Joel 2:10; 3:14-16). Malachi 4:5 speaks like all the fore-mentioned prophets about the "great and dreadful day of the Lord." All these prophets, nonetheless, had in their prophecies a line of hope running through them. The line was an assurance that the Day of the Lord will not just be judgment but there will also be mercy for those who have put their trust in the Lord.

The prophets foretold of the day when the Lord would come and rescue Israel from her tormentors. This will be a day when all the redeemed of the Lord will enter into their rest. On this day, God would intervene in human history and avenge the cruelty perpetrated on those who have been called by God over the years. The imagery is the same in nearly all the prophecies that speak of this day. The prophecies concerning the signs in the heaven generally speak of the moon, the sun, and the stars ceasing to shine. Amos calls it a day of darkness not light (Amos 5:20). This day is called a "vengeful day." Isaiah, Jeremiah, and Ezekiel speak of bloodshed, while other prophets allude to it. The word for day in Hebrew is *yom* meaning a literal 24 hour day or an unspecified period of time; therefore, it is unclear as to the length of this "day."

The people of Israel believed that the Messiah would usher this day in, but most of them did not understand that the Messiah would first die for human sin. The promise in the prophets was the coming of Messiah, the destruction of the enemies of Israel, and the re-establishment of the glory of Israel. Since the threat of annihilation by Assyria, the prophets had proclaimed the "day of the Lord." Obadiah mentions, "For the day of the Lord upon all the nations is near; As you have done it shall be done to you. Your reprisal shall return upon your own head" (Obadiah 1:15). The key in this is that God will come for the people who call upon the name of the Lord. The God who called Israel will surely intervene in the situation of the people. Evil shall not ultimately triumph over the called of God. Israel, though whipped and subjugated, will experience the salvation of the God. God's day of deliverance will surely come.

The Gospels

The Gospel of Matthew records Jesus speaking about His return. In chapter 24, His disciples ask Him about the sign of His coming. Jesus mentions famines, wars, and pestilence (24:7), but says that these are the "beginning of sorrows." He speaks of great tribulation and the rise of false prophets and a false Christ (Matthew 24:15-28). But in verse 29 Jesus alludes to the same description as Isaiah, Jeremiah, and Joel. He describes the sun and the moon failing to give off their light and the stars falling from heaven. This is the major sign of His appearing.

In verses 36-44, Jesus explains that no one knows when this will take place. The story of Noah is used to illustrate that just as people were drinking and marrying, the floods came without warning (except to Noah and his family) and brought destruction. Therefore, the Son of man will return when you least expect it (24:44), and He will bring judgment. In Luke 21:25-36, Jesus speaks about His return. He mentions that there will be signs in the heavens but this description is not as specific as in Matthew.

Mark records Jesus' response to the disciples' question about His return in chapter 13. This account is basically the same as Matthew, the sun darkens, the moon fails to give light, and the stars fall from the sky. Mark also mentions that the "Son of man will come in the clouds in great power and glory" (Mark 13:26). All these accounts echo the declarations of the Old Testament prophets. They speak of a day or time of judgment. The difference in the Gospels is that Jesus is identified as the avenger of which the prophets spoke. John does not record a conversation about "the day of the Lord." However, John chapter 14 does record Jesus telling the disciples that He must go away but that He would return get them and take them to be with Him. Of course, John would later write the Book of Revelation, and there he would speak more specifically about the end times.

Paul is the only apostle, beside Peter and Jude, who actually writes about the Day of the Lord. Most of what Paul had to say is found in 1 and 2 Thessalonians. Paul mentions the Day of the Lord in 1 Corinthians 5:5. This verse is in regard to an immoral brother in Corinth who had sexual relations with his father's wife. Paul tells the church to turn him over to Satan that his soul may be saved in the Day of the Lord. Another brief mention can also be found in 2 Corinthians 1:14 in which Paul speaks about boasting about the Corinthians in the Day of the Lord.

Paul mentions the Day of the Lord in 1 Thessalonians 5 and says that it will come like a "thief in the night." He also mentions the sudden destruction that will over take people speaking about "peace and safety." In chapter 4, he mentions Jesus' coming, but many scholars believe this refers to "being caught up"or "the rapture" of the church. In 2 Thessalonians 2, Paul writes to correct the notion that the Day of the Lord had already come. He mentions that "the man of lawlessness" must be revealed first. He then explains how when Jesus returns He will destroy the man of lawlessness by His coming.

The Book of Acts records what is believed to be the first sermon of the infant church at the day of Pentecost. Peter stands with the other apostles and preaches, quoting Joel 2:28-32. In this quote, Peter speaks of heaven with reference to the state of the sun and the moon. Acts 2:20 says that the "sun will turn to darkness and the moon to blood," before "the great and glorious day of the Lord" (NIV). The Book of Jude mentions scoffers in the last days (v. 17), as well as angels being kept in chains for judgment until "the great day."

Peter now recalls all the information that had been spoken or written before his epistle in 2 Peter. He mentions the false prophets and teachers that Jesus spoke of and alludes to the flood in 3:6, as Jesus did in Matthew 24. Peter probably recalls Jesus' words when he says in 3:10a the "day of the Lord will come like a thief in the night." In 3:10b-13 Peter speaks of many destructive events which will take place in the heavens alluding to what was spoken by the prophets. But in these prophesies, the believer must remember that this will happen because God is coming to deliver God's people from all their oppression and bondage. In the world, it has never been heard that anyone held in bondage either by human powers or demonic powers were released without struggle. The Day of the Lord will result in a final deliverance of all God's people.

The Problem of the Perceived Delay of Jesus' Return

Peter's second epistle was written approximately 30 years after Jesus' death and resurrection. Many believers felt that Christ would not come in their lifetime. Thus, they were discouraged and began to believe that He would never return for them. It must be remembered that this was more than just belief. Among believers of the first century, this delay implied that evil will triumph after all. For them, it meant that all their labors were in vain and that they had suffered in vain. Some of them interpreted Jesus' words in Matthew 24:34, "This generation will certainly not pass away until all these things have happened" (NIV), to refer to their own generation. But scholars have interpreted this statement to refer not to the people He was talking to and their generation, but the generation in which these signs begin to occur. This would mean that Jesus' return could take place anytime in the future, unlike the other interpretation that would mean Christ would have to return before the end of that particular generation. The problem of the people to whom Peter was writing is that instead of focusing on the fact that Jesus will come for them, they focused on when He was going to come.

Many in the early church were looking for Christ to return in their generation. As time went by and saints began to die or be martyred, people became anxious. Persecution caused the early Christians to believe that they were in the last days. In Matthew 24:36, Jesus tells His disciples that no one knows the day or the hour, not even the Son knows. Only the Father knows the time of Jesus' return. Yet they could not keep themselves from interpreting the times and speculating about the return of the Master. By setting their hearts on time, they made themselves open to discouragement. To keep ourselves from such discouragement all we need to know is that the Lord will surely come for us and that He will not disappoint us.

Peter's way of dealing with the brothers and sisters of his time was to remind them that God stands outside of time. He says in 2 Peter 3:8 that a day is like a thousand years, and a thousand years are like a day in the sight of the Lord. His emphasis is that God is not bound by time nor is the Lord as concerned about it as we might be. God is only bound by the promise to return for us. However, Peter does say that when Christ comes, it will be like a "thief in the night." In other words when you least expect it, Christ will appear. But we must be ready. We must never give up expecting the appearance of our Lord and Master. Paul states that Christians should be ready and not be caught unaware (1 Thessalonians 5:2-5). The implication is that even though we do not know when Christ will return, we know that He will, and we shouldn't be surprised when He appears. However, those who don't know Christ will be surprised.

One of the problems that arises for us as human beings when there is delay of any sort is that our first tendency is the expression of disappointment. Then there arises anger, following anger there is the outgrowth of cynicism. All these may lead to a verbal attack or as Peter calls it "scoffing." Because of the perceived delay of the Lord's coming, many Christians became disappointed and some even turned away and began to mock what they had previously believed. It's one thing to deal with scoffers who have never believed. The scoffers who had known the truth but are now on the enemy camp are much more difficult to deal with. They can quote the Bible, they can recite history, and they can philosophize about the increase of evil in the world. Even though there may be many who scoff at us because we believe that our Lord will come for us, we must not give up expecting the hour of His appearance. Peter says there were scoffers in his day. These scoffers did not stop Peter from waiting for the coming of his soul's redemption. The word for "scoffers" in the Greek could better be translated "mockers." These were people who made fun of or made sport of those who believed in the return of Christ. These mockers were not just unbelievers. Among them were many backsliders. These "mockers" had a field day making fun of Christians who were waiting for Christ to appear and deliver them from all their sufferings. Even some believers began to doubt that Jesus was going to appear just as He left. They began to spiritualize the second coming of the Lord. When we perceive that there is delay in the timing of what God has promised, then we ought be aware of the ungodly behavior of false prophets who may seek to lead us into the error of their teaching.

The problem with these scoffers is that they tend to place themselves on par with God by questioning the character of God and the time of divine activity. One of the manifestations is that people begin to question why good people die or why they suffer. "Why does Jesus not return and change things before all these good patriarchs and matriarchs of the faith fall into the sleep of death?" they ask (v. 4). Part of the reason given by Peter for why people turn into scoffing and cynicism is their motivation. In the days of Peter, he says that these people were moved by selfish and evil desires (v. 3). Many wanted to set themselves up as the true bearer of the message of the Christ. When there is delay, false teachers can easily prey upon our vulnerability. In times of delay, people tend to give themselves to rumor-mongering. Delays tends to cause us as human beings to exaggerate whatever suffering it is that we are experiencing. This exaggeration leads to wishful thinking. Then we tend to distort the Word of God and sometimes downright disobey it. As a result of this perceived delay, people began to say that Jesus had already returned (2 Thessalonians 2). All this confusion arises because of the unwillingness of the people to wait for God's timing and trust in God's faithfulness.

As in the day of Peter, the delay in the second coming of Jesus can be a great ammunition for the skeptics who cannot find in their heart to believe in the triumph of good over evil. Yet, the believer should not be disheartened or discouraged. It was the same as in the delay of the flood during Noah's time. Noah preached for a number of years while he built the ark and he was mocked until the rain began to fall. Yet, the ark was built and the rain did come, and Noah and all those who believed were saved. As God came to Noah to save him from the flood, God will come for you. As God came for Israel in the land of Egypt, God will come for you. As God came for Jesus in the tomb after three days, God will come for you.

Persecution and the seeming power of the evil over the good makes our sense of delay get the better of us. Many in Peter's time joined the scoffers and cynics because of the depth of persecution. "Surely," it was thought, "God cannot stand back and watch such suffering." But the truth is that many lack knowledge of the Scripture. Jesus made it clear that suffering and persecution are part of the mark of His followers. "If you were of the world, the world would love its own. But you are not of this world, therefore the world hates you"(John 15:19). But one thing He has promised you is that He will be with you and will come for you. You cannot fail for waiting for Him. Even He Himself had to wait for three days in the grave, yet death and evil never triumphed over Him. God did not suffer Him to see corruption. Therefore, even though persecution is intensified against us, we cannot give up. We must not stop anticipating the coming of our Saviour. In the days of Peter, though persecution was not at its highest level, some saints were still martyred for their faith. This led many to stop believing that the Lord would come again. During this period, Stephen had been stoned to death (35 A.D.); James was killed by a sword (42 A.D.); there was the persecution of Christians in Palestine (52 A.D.); Paul was arrested (58 A.D.); James the Just (brother of Jesus) is martyred (62 A.D.); and Peter and Paul were believed to be sentenced to death under emperor Nero (65 A.D.) All these may seem disheartening and could have caused Peter to become discouraged like many believers of his time, yet he was able to remind his sisters and brothers of the faithfulness of the Lord who called. Because of such persecution, suffering, and death, many may flee the church; many may leave the holy city, the Jerusalem of God, for the worldly city of Rome. Yes, for a brief period, the worldly city may seem a safe harbor, and for a while the city of God may seem deserted. But remember that the city of God is an everlasting city, its builder is God and God never fails. In the worldly city, a Paul maybe a prisoner but his freedom is stronger than the chains that bind him. He is confident because he knows that the Lord will come for him. Peter may come to Rome under the threat of death, but he knows that though his Lord does not come to deliver him, surely he will see the triumph of his Master over the stakes and fire of dying Rome. Zealots of unbelief may now cause problems for the church, but we know that the promise of the Lord is sure. False teachers and scoffers may align themselves with forces of evil in our time of waiting, but they cannot overcome us, for we know that Jesus our Lord and Master will come for us. Our claim of victory is secure in the hand of the everlasting God. Just as the church of the first century continued to thrive, showing the power of the Lord, we who wait for the Lord today, know that no matter how bad it gets, though Jesus does not come physically, He is always present spiritually, and He will come physically someday for us.

Be Steadfast

The key to steadfastness is to know the presence of our Lord is with us. The angel of God's presence is always there to help us in times of turmoil and radical change, even when the changes do not seem to be in our favor (Numbers 10:21). In fact, Paul maintains that the important thing, whether we are at home with the Lord, in heaven, or with God spiritually as we are now in the flesh, is always to live in the presence of God. God desires always to be in our midst. Even in our problems, God's presence is sure (Psalm 34:18-19; 140:12). God is always encountering people wherever they may be and in whatever situation they may find themselves. The appearance of the Day of the Lord will mean nothing if we are not now in the presence of the Lord.

Look into the face of the Lord, for our God is always present with us. In the Old Testament the prophets who spoke of the "day of the Lord" did not merely wait for that day to order their lives in the light of God's face. They saw God's presence as continual. They knew that the God, who used a variety of revelational means to communicate with the people of God, was still present (Genesis 15:1; 32:24-30). If we have a close relationship with God like Moses had, encountering God "face to face" (Deuteronomy 34:10) will not frighten us, for we are already in the heart of God. Though we know that Jesus will come physically to receive the Church, we must never forget that the primary and tangible symbol of God's presence with the people of Israel was the Ark of the Covenant. We who are "the temple of the Lord," as Paul says, are now the tangible presence of the Lord till He comes again.

We are the container of the Lord's glory on this earth "though we have this treasure in earthen vessels" (2 Corinthians 4:7), we have it nonetheless. God has set the divine throne in the hearts of those who believe. As in the Old Testament, the presence of God in our hearts and in God's Church continues to lead us to meet our God on the great Day. In the desert with Israel and Elijah's life, the presence of God was manifested in fire (1 Kings 18). Today that fire burns in our hearts through the presence of the Holy Spirit who came to the Church in tongues of fire. The presence of the Lord came to Elijah in a still small voice (1 Kings 19). Today we can still hear the Lord's voice in our souls, speaking to us gently and leading us into the great Day as we wait for the coming of the Lord. The Lord always comes to His people. God still addresses us as He addressed the ancestors. God addressed Ezekiel's exiled community and came to them in divine glory (Ezekiel 43:1-5). We know that the Lord of Israel came to us in Emmanuel, "God with us" (Matthew 1:23; John 1:14; Hebrews 1:1-3). The Scriptures are clear that this presence did not end with the death of Christ. After rising from death, the Lord came to the disciples several times (John 21:1-14). When Paul was groping in the night of hatred, the Lord came to him and for him. The key is not to let the coming of the Lord in judgment distract from seeing the coming of the Lord in mercy. By coming to Paul on the road to Damascus, Christ continued the work He came to do (Acts 1:8; 26:12-18). In His presence the redemptive work of God continues. These are signs that there will be a return which will bring fulfillment and divine presence which will be permanent. For then God shall be the everlasting light of the people.

The problem with the people to whom Peter wrote and with some of us is that we concentrate on the last and final coming; we forget the continual coming of the Lord into the lives of thousands which is what makes the Second Coming so exciting! The most exciting thing about the Second Coming is not that God is going to zap our enemies but that thousands upon thousands will have obtained mercy. It will be moving to see the millions, into whose heart the Lord has come and made His abode. Think about that "great gettin' up morning." Praise the Lord. Think of the miracle of the reconstitution of the destroyed body. Think of it, the hearty laughter of those whom the enemy thought he had defeated forever. Think of the fallen rising up and staring our archenemy, the devil, in the face and declaring victory. But only those who have won victory in this spiritual coming of the Lord will experience the victory in the final coming of the Lord. The Lord is coming for you. Be ready.

How Is the Believer to Deal with This Sense of Delay?
Trust God's Word

If He will come for us, we must keep our mind stayed on Him now. The key of experiencing Him joyfully at His Second Coming is to maintain an attitude of praise. Peter says that things have not remained the same since the patriarchs died. God sent a flood to destroy the world. Peter reiterates that by God's Word heaven and earth were created (v. 5) and by God's Word they are reserved for judgment by fire. If God kept His word and brought destruction by water, the Lord can be trusted to keep His word in regard to the final judgment, the Day of the Lord.

When there is delay, or a perceived delay as we find among the people to whom Peter wrote, and people begin to scoff, it may be due to the fact that they no longer trust God's Word. Abraham must have seemed like a fool to his contemporaries for waiting so long for God to give him the land that had been promised. But he trusted in the word of the Lord who will not lie (Genesis 15:1-17). If the people of Sodom and Gomorrah had only chosen to trust in the word of God which came to them through Lot and then the angels, they would not have been destroyed (Genesis 18:1-20). Isaac was given to Sarah after a long period of what may have seemed an unnecessary delay on the part of God in human sight, but at the right time the promise of the Lord was fulfilled (Genesis 21:1-23). We are told that only those who walk by faith will experience the actualization of God's power (Hebrews 11:1-40). The question then is not so much whether the Lord will come but whether we believe that God's promise is true. Furthermore, we must ask whether we are willing to wait for it, hold on to it, and stake our very life on the fact that one day the trumpet shall resound, the Lord shall descend (1 Thessaloniasn 4:16), and that, in fact, it will be well with our souls.

We can trust in the coming of the Lord because God is not interested in making us stake our lives on half-truths. It may be difficult to continue trusting when nothing seems to happen (Genesis 30:22-24). It may be difficult when we have to face new situations and we cannot seem to find an anchor in the storm. It may be difficult when we have everything going for us and we can see how, through our human ways, we may be able to solve our situation. We even have the power to destroy those who persecute us, but God tells us to be still. God says, "Vengeance is mine. I will repay" (Romans 12:19b). It may be difficult when, like Joseph, we are accused falsely and we seem to wait in vain for the deliverance which was promised and it does not come when we think it should come (Genesis 50:5). Yet in all these circumstances, we must trust in God's promises (Genesis 50:24). We should, in all of our situations, hear the Apostle Paul say, "Yea in all these thing we are more than conquerors, through Him" (Romans 8:37). We are called to trust God who will make sure that those who oppress us will give an account (Exodus 2:9). Besides, those of us who trust the Lord know that not trusting God is to find ourselves, as they say, "up a creek without a paddle." Here we are really called to exercise a childlike faith as we believe that God will ultimately come for us. Mark 10:14 captures the problem with the people of Peter's day. They worried more about what God will do in the last days than they did about their own lives and their relationship with God. Such worrying about "last things," as some call it, can affect our trust in the Word of

God (Matthew 6:34). When we worry so much about what will happen in the last day, does not that mean that we really lack confidence that Christ will keep us unto Himself until the day of His appearing? We who wait for the coming, believe that the Lord will come for us because we believe in the everlasting strength of God (Isaiah 26:4). We believe that our God will come for us, for the goodness of God is everlasting and this goodness dictates that the Lord comes for His own. As Scripture says, God's loving-kindness is everlasting (Psalm 36:7). The richness of God's mercy and the overflowing nature of the same leads me to believe that God will come for me. God will come for us because God cares.

Do Not Confuse Human Time with God's Timing

Part of what creates a problem for those who wait for the coming of the Lord is the fact that we tend to confuse our view of time with God's view of time. God stands outside of time. The divine is not constrained to 24 hours a day, nor 7 days a week. Peter also indicates that God is not slow in keeping His promise. The word for "slow" could be translated "tardy" as if God were behind schedule, or late for work. The fact is that our Father is always on time. If there seems to be a delay, we must see it mainly as a manifestation of God's patience. If God was in a hurry like many of us are, then many of us would be condemned because the Lord would have come before we had the opportunity to turn to God. The word for patient is "longsuffering" in the King James Version. What may seem to us like delay may mean that God continues to show that there is hope and that God does not lose heart concerning our salvation. God's patience means that our Lord can patiently bear the offenses and injuries of others far more than we can. God is waiting for everyone who will repent to repent. In 1 Timothy 2:3-4, Paul says: "This is good, and pleases God our Savior, who wants all men to be saved and to come to a knowledge of the truth" (NIV). Though this statement is in regard to praying for those in authority, it illustrates the fact that what we call delay may be tied to God's patience which desires everyone to be saved. God is patiently waiting for all to come to repentance and, therefore, withholds the judgment until He deems it time. Only God knows when that is, and it is not on our schedule. The truth is that God will come not mainly to destroy but to receive as many as would believe in the name of the Lord Jesus Christ. There may seem to be a delay, but at the right time, our God will come in power. Trust the Lord; remember that a thousand years are but a day in the sight of God, so wait. God will come for you.

Peter says in verse 10, "The day of the Lord will come like a thief in the night." The emphasis is on the word "will." In verse 10, Peter makes four assertions: (1) The Day of the Lord will come; (2) The heavens will disappear; (3) The elements will be destroyed by fire; (4) Everything will be laid bare. These assertions are made because God is faithful. This means that God, who promised to come for His Church, is steadfast, dependable, and worthy of trust. This is the same root that gives us the word "amen." The derived meaning is that the one so described is trustworthy, dependable, trusting, or loyal. Moses was faithful in all God's household (Numbers 12:7). "Faithful" is used to describe the relationship between God and Israel (Deuteronomy 7:9). This the faithful God who keeps covenant with the divinely chosen people. When we say that God is faithful we are at the very least saying that God maintains fidelity toward us. God will not betray. The same God whom the Bible says is "faithful and just to forgive us our sins, and to cleanse us from all unrighteousness" (1 John 1:9) is the God who promised to come for us. This God says Paul "is faithful, who will not suffer you to be tempted above that ye are able" (1 Corinthians 10:13). At another place he says, "Faithful is he that calleth you, who also will do it" (1 Thessalonians 5:24). Our faithful God is steadfast, unchanging, forever committed to us. God will come seeking for us. From generation to generation, God has kept promises. God kept the promise to deliver Noah from the flood; He will also keep the promise to come and take you unto Himself. God has promised to come back for you and to reach for you even beyond the grave. If God has promised that Jesus will return to receive you unto Himself and to give you final victory, it *will* happen. No power, no authority, no scoffers, no false teacher, no earthly or heavenly being or element can stop Him from coming for you and filling you completely with divine bounty. Our Lord is the One who said, "Do not let your hearts be troubled. Believe in God, believe also in me. In my Father's house there are many dwelling places, if it were not so, would I have told you that I go to prepare a place for you?" (John 14:2, paraphrased) The Master, He will come for you. You are God's, and you will spend eternity in victory with God's Son.

Chapter Seven

ON BEING LOYAL TO JESUS AS LORD

John 13:37-38

Peter said unto him, Lord, why cannot I follow thee now? I will lay down my life for thy sake. [38]Jesus answered him, Wilt thou lay down thy life for my sake? Verily, verily, I say unto thee, The cock shall not crow, till thou hast denied me thrice.

John 18:25-27

And Simon Peter stood and warmed himself. They said therefore unto him, Art not thou also one of his disciples? He denied it, and said, I am not. [26]One of the servants of the high priest, being his kinsman whose ear Peter cut off, saith, Did not I see thee in the garden with him? [27]Peter then denied again: and immediately the cock crew.

John 21:15-25

So when they had dined, Jesus saith to Simon Peter, Simon, son of Jonas, lovest thou me more than these? He saith unto him, Yea, Lord: thou knowest that I love thee. He saith unto him, Feed my lambs. [16]He saith to him again the second time, Simon, son of Jonas, lovest thou me? He saith unto him, Yea, Lord; thou knowest that I love thee. He saith unto him, Feed my sheep. [17]He saith unto him the third time, Simon, son of Jonas, lovest thou me? Peter was grieved because he said unto him the third time, Lovest thou me? And he said unto him, Lord, thou knowest all things; thou knowest that I love thee. Jesus saith unto him, Feed my sheep. [18]Verily, verily, I say unto thee, When thou wast young, thou girdest thyself, and walkest whither thou wouldest: but when thou shalt be old, thou shalt stretch forth thy hands, and another shall gird thee, and carry thee whither thou wouldest not. [19]This spake he, signifying by what death he should glorify God. And when he had spoken this, he saith unto him, Follow me. [20]Then Peter, turning about, seeth the disciple whom Jesus loved following; which also leaned on his breast at supper, and said, Lord, which is he that betrayeth thee? [21]Peter seeing him saith to Jesus, Lord, and what shall this man do? [22]Jesus saith unto him, If I will that he tarry till I come, what is that to thee? follow thou me. [23]Then went this saying abroad among the brethren, that disciple should not die: yet Jesus said not unto him, He shall not die; but, If I will that he tarry till I come, what is that to thee? [24]This is the disciple which testifieth of these things, and wrote these things: and we know that his testimony is true. [25]And there are also many other things which Jesus did, the which, if they should be written every one, I suppose that even the world itself could not contain the books that should be written. Amen.

John 13:37-38—This incident takes place in the Upper Room. Jesus has washed the disciples feet, explained the significance of it, identified Judas as the one who will betray Him, and commanded them to love one another as a way of keeping them together and making an impact on the world. He then informs them of His soon departure. Peter asked Jesus where He was going (v. 36). Jesus replied that he (Peter) could not go, but that later he would follow. Jesus was referring to His death on the cross. He said that Peter would follow because He knew that one day Peter would be crucified and killed by Roman soldiers. Peter, unaware of what Jesus was talking about, declared that he was willing to die for Jesus. Then Jesus predicted that Peter would deny Him three times before the "rooster" crows.

John 18:25-27—Following the Upper Room events (chs. 13 17) Jesus is arrested and taken to Annas. This man had held the title of high priest from A.D. 6 to A.D. 15 when Valerius Gratus, governor of Judea, deposed him. Though Caiaphas was the official high priest at the time, Annas held more influence and still retained the title of high priest. It is at the hearing before Caiaphas that Peter's denials take place. The first denial is recorded in verse 17. Peter is confronted by a slave girl who asked if he was a disciple. Peter replied that he was not. The next two denials are recorded in verses 25-26. In verse 25, he is asked again if he is a disciple. His answer is, "no!" The final question relates to his whereabouts. He is recognized as one who was in the garden with Jesus. When asked if he was there, he denies it. We are told that "at that moment a rooster began to crow" (v. 26, NIV). The account of Peters' denial of Jesus is recounted in each Gospel. In all the Gospels except John, Peter weeps bitterly after the rooster crows. It should also be noted that Peter never denied Jesus as Lord, he denied association with Him. Peter was willing to follow Jesus, but not unto death.

John 21:15-19—This scene takes place shortly after the disciples have been fishing. It has been suggested that John added this last event "to clear up a misunderstanding that had arisen regarding Jesus' words concerning the future of the beloved disciple and to record the restoration of Simon Peter to a position of unique responsibility within the Church" (David Ellis, *The International Bible Commentary,* Zondervan Publishing House, p. 1263). Jesus appeared to them and told them to cast their nets on the right side of the boat to catch fish. It is after they have finished eating their catch that Jesus asks Peter three questions.

The first question Jesus asked Peter was if he loved Jesus "more than these." Peter answered positively, adding "you know I love you." Jesus commissioned him to "feed my lambs." The second question is the same as the first except the phrase "more than these" is eliminated. Peter's response is the same. This time Jesus commissions Peter, "Take care of my sheep" (v.16, NIV). The third question is the same as the second but Peter is now "hurt." The Greek word translated "hurt" (v. 17, NIV) carries the idea of feeling "sorrow" or "sadness." Hence, Peter having been asked this question twice, is now saddened that Jesus would ask it again. Peter answered that Jesus knows all things, and knows that Peter loves Him. The Greek word translated "know" which Peter uses in each of his answers, refers to knowledge perceived with the eyes or gained by insight. Peter has been stating that just as Jesus knew he would deny Him, so Jesus also knew Peter loved Him.

With the confession of his love and allegiance to Jesus, Peter is ready for his new mission. He who once denied association with Jesus would soon lead the flock. At Pentecost, he would preach the first sermon (Acts 14). He would be the first to take the Gospel to the Gentiles (Acts 10). He would write two epistles (1 and 2 Peter). He would, according to tradition, help Mark write his Gospel. Then he would fulfill the prediction of Jesus and follow Him into eternity. He would be crucified (according to tradition) upside down in Rome around 64 A.D. under Emperor Nero.

The Meaning of Loyalty

To be loyal is to maintain a certain consistency in our commitment to someone, in this case God and Jesus the Son of God. Loyalty is not something one can obtain through coercion (2 Chronicles 11:1). In fact, Proverbs 3:3 reminds us of the importance of loyalty. In the Book of John, Jesus calls

His disciples friends. Friendship is sealed by loyalty. It is by the depth of one's loyalty that true friendship is determined (Proverbs 17:17). Our primary loyalty must be with God (Matthew 6:33). In all this we know that loyalty simply means a wholehearted devotion to something or someone. The American philosopher, Josiah Royce once said that loyalty is "the willing and thoroughgoing devotion of a person to a cause." He also argued that it is a commitment to something greater than one's private affections. To be loyal is to commit oneself to something beyond one's ego and to love that commitment deeply. But we are not always loyal or our loyalty is fleeting; that is, we allow it to be affected negatively by time or circumstances. Some of us are loyal only if it suits us. Loyalty is far less prevalent today than it used to be.

Loyalty is connected to love. In fact, it can be interchanged with love. For just as friendship cannot survive without loyalty, it cannot survive without expression of love. Loyalty grows out of the feeling of intimate connection with one another. But does our world know what loyalty means? By the way many relationships in our world go, especially marriage, it would seem that we have lost the true meaning of loyalty. When two people get married, they pledge to serve, honor, love and cherish each other for richer, for poorer, in sickness, and in health, for better or worse, forsaking all others, as long as they both shall live. This promise of loyalty sounds great, doesn't it? But you and I know that 50 percent of these marriages will not survive. And yet many of the surviving marriages yield examples of couples who have stayed together through "thick and thin" and have been blessed immeasurable because of it. Loyalty pays. We move from church to church, from friend to friend, not because we need to grow or that we are obeying a greater or higher loyalty, but because we fail to understand the benefits of genuine loyalty. Sometimes even loyalty to God takes back seat because we have either misplaced our loyalty on other things which really do not matter or because we cannot at the present moment understand the benefit of this loyalty.

In the passage of Scripture which serves as the background to this study, Peter, like many of us, pledged his loyalty to his friend and Master Jesus, saying, "Lord I will follow you wherever you go." Peter, in making that statement, did not really understand the demand this loyalty to the Master will put upon him. At the time of the promise, he did not understand that his loyalty would be tested. He did not understand that he may fail to exhibit the faithfulness which his pledge of loyalty demands. He was too quick to promise his loyalty to the Lord Jesus Christ, but his loyalty could not stand the test of time. Thankfully, Jesus does not abandon His disciples, even when their loyalty seems shaken because of the bad experiences which happen so often in our world. Jesus seeks His disciples out as He sought for Peter. Though we may fail in our loyalty and promise of love, Jesus is willing to restore us as He restored Peter to His fellowship and friendship. His loyalty to us is amazing. When Peter's promise of loyalty failed, Jesus reassured him. Jesus also reminded him that one way to rebuild his loyalty was to practice loyalty in feeding the flock which He was about to commit to Peter. His loyalty was now going to be measured by the way in which he served as the under-shepherd of Christ which he was intended to be. We can and should learn from Peter's pledge of loyalty to Jesus, his failure, and his restoration to fellowship with the Lord. Everyday we should pledge or renew our loyalty to our God. Through continuous prayer, we can express our desire to be loyal, completely devoted to the Lord. God can empower us to be totally devoted to the lordship of Jesus.

Declared Loyalty to Jesus is Just the Beginning (John 13:37-38)

Peter declared his loyalty to the Lord Jesus when he boldly asserted, "I will lay down my life for you." This declaration is occasioned by Jesus' statement that He is about to leave them and go to a place where they could not come now. Whether Jesus is referring to His death or the glorification which would follow His death is not clear. In either case, Jesus indicated Peter could not follow Him at that time. Peter's statement that he is prepared to die for his Master suggests he thought Jesus might be headed for trouble and he is ready to give his own life in defense of his Friend. The pledge of loyalty from Peter did not mean that he was perfect. Peter did not know that his own weakness would get the better of him and lead him to deny the Lord. Yet this, his declaration of loyalty, shows what is needed for anyone who will follow the Lord. His decision was well-intentioned.

On the other hand, when we declare our loyalty to Jesus, it is always incomplete. Our declaration is impoverished by the limitation of our understanding. This does not mean that it is not good. It just means that we, like Peter, speak from our dark glasses and cannot see all that our declaration of loyalty entails. But we must declare our loyalty to the One who brings to us the message of life. In that one declaration is encoded many of the wonderful things which will later unfold for us as we continue to reaffirm our loyalty to God. This calls to mind the experience of Israel in the desert when Moses gave them the Law. They declared that they will serve the Lord. Yet we know that this declaration did not make them immune to all the problems of the desert. Notwithstanding their declaration, they still had to face foreign gods in the desert. They still had to trust God through the desert. They still had to carry the parts of the temple. Every declaration of loyalty must be tested. Though our declaration of loyalty immediately puts us into the camp of God, this did not mean we immediately acquire all the wealth available to those who are committed to God. The Israelites still had to dig; they still had to walk to the Promised Land. They still had to conquer the land. But many of them, like Peter, confused their declaration with attainment. They thought that just because they said it, they no longer needed to pray, wait, or work. What happens to many of us who have declared our loyalty to Jesus is that we rest on our laurels and become overly absorbed with our sense of security. But Peter, in his declaration, did not know that his declaration was just the beginning; he did not seem to understand that the seed must be pushed into the ground, sometimes even beaten to the ground. He was so caught up in his declaration of loyalty that he did not see that the seed must endure the dark night of the soil, the drenching wetness of the rainy season, and maybe even the humidity and heat causing it to rot from the outside and become so uncomfortable that it is forced to grow out of itself. In this process, we must understand that loyalty is more than words. What happens when we declare our loyalty to the Lord is that we have just framed the context for our own growth. We have just put up a sign that says, "I belong." We have just made a faith.

A declaration of loyalty is made under the assumption of the open possibilities which are promised by the one to whom we are dedicated. In many respects, to make a declaration of loyalty is to enter into a reciprocal relationship with the divine. When we declare our loyalty to Jesus, it affects and influences the direction of our lives. To declare is not just to talk about it; it is not just to develop a way of speaking about something to which one is unwilling to commit. It is to enter into the divine pathos. Our declaration of loyalty means that from now on we are no longer independent or mainly concerned about our individualism but that we are now willing to attend to the things of God and ignore or refuse all other claims upon our lives. This declaration of loyalty helps to shape and define our whole spiritual existence. Thus when Peter declares his loyalty in the presence of Jesus, he is promising to let the Lord form and structure his spiritual landscape. He was saying that his ultimate and his highest now belongs to Jesus. Even his life in that moment of declaration no longer belonged to him but to the Lord. For he said "I will even lay down my life for you."

Peter's declaration of loyalty derives from the depth of his relationship with the Master. Those of us who want to develop loyalty to the Lord can only do so if we have entered into a relationship with Him. We must listen, walk closely with Him, and love Him. It is impossible to be loyal where there is not a relationship. We must develop a relationship with Jesus if we are to be loyal to Him. We cannot be truly loyal to anyone whom we have not known. Such attachment is mere sentimental romanticism. True loyalty is deeper than that. It is dedication of the total self. By listening to Jesus, Peter had come to know him pretty well. Peter had listened to Jesus' teaching and concluded that He was no ordinary teacher. The truth of which Jesus spoke touched the core of Peter's heart like no one he had heard.

Loyalty may be defined as the quality of being dedicated or faithful to a cause, an institution, or a person. Dedication to a person is usually a quality built up over a period of time, and the result of weighing the worth of the person to whom one becomes attached. By declaring his loyalty, Peter was now dedicating his life to the Master. Dedication comes through careful consideration of several factors. In Jesus, he saw the manifestation of the kingdom of God as in power and in truth. Eldon Ladd defines the kingdom of God as "the sovereign rule of God manifested in Christ to defeat His enemies, creating a people over whom He reigns, and issuing in a realm, or realms in which the power of His reign is experienced" (*Zondervan Pictorial Bible Dictionary*, p. 466). By hearing Jesus announce that He had come to proclaim the kingdom, something within Peter was moved to commit his life to Him. This loyalty was grounded on the conviction that, through Jesus, God would ultimately reclaim creation, and reassert divine authority over all. Given the fact that Peter was among the lower class of his day, the idea that God would finally institute the redemptive plan for Israel and that Peter would be one of the citizens of this kingdom spurred deep longing within him. This longing, of course, responded to the call for repentance and acceptance of Christ as Messiah.

Loyalty Comes through Knowledge of Jesus

Peter was not being loyal to something he did not know, for Jesus clearly defined for him and fellow disciples the nature of this new community (Matthew 13; John 3:3-5). He knew the cost and as well as the requirements for discipleship to be a part of this new community (Luke 14:25-34). He knew that this demanded a total commitment (Matthew 5-7). Peter had seen Jesus communicate the message through sermons that were so powerful they moved the soul of all who heard Him (Matthew 5-7), parables (Matthew 13), stories (Luke 15), dialogue with Jewish leaders (John 5-7), etc. It was in the process of being so privy to this teaching that Peter began to develop loyalty. Jesus through mode of communicating the truth entered into a deep relationship with Peter and thus became worthy of this strong-headed disciple's loyalty.

Another way of developing loyalty to Jesus is not by just listening to teaching but by experiencing Him first-hand through the wonder that He does. The many miracles Jesus performed served as "signs." That is, they served to back up His teachings as authentic and God-given. Among the variety of miracles Peter saw Jesus perform, the following can be noted. He saw Jesus drive out evil spirits (Mark 1:21-28; 5:1-20), heal people, including his mother-in-law, of a variety of afflictions (Mark 1:29-34; 3:1-6), raise the dead (Mark 5:38-43), feed multitudes (John 6), and walk on water (Mark 6:47-50). He also saw Jesus transfigured on the mountain, and heard the voice from the clouds say, "This is my Son, whom I love. Listen to him" (Mark 9:2-12, NIV). In some of these miracles, Peter, James, and John are the only disciples present, perhaps the intent of Jesus was to convince them of His identity and to build loyalty. These miracles would have helped to convince Peter that Jesus was worthy of his devotion, and would have contributed to his emotional outburst that he was ready to die for Jesus. Teachings are impressive. Miracles are impressive. But character further authenticates the worth of an individual. Jesus' character was impeccable.

Why Be Loyal to Jesus?

Our loyalty to Jesus derives from His character as a man of *integrity*. There was no hint of hypocrisy or duplicity in His dealings with people. He did not say one thing and do another. He did not tell His disciples to "do as I say do, not as I do" as some modern leaders are reported to say. Jesus was genuine, the same all the time. He did not have a private lifestyle different from His public lifestyle.

Our loyalty to Jesus is grounded in His character as a man of *courage.* Many people in our day would like folks to be loyal to them even when they refuse to stand up for what is right. But not so with Jesus. It is the fact that Jesus was not afraid to suffer for His conviction that allows us to know that our loyalty to Him is well-deserved. He did not hesitate to confront the religious leaders of His day when their teachings and practices contradicted God's will (Matthew 23). He drove those from the temple who sought to make it a place for business when it was intended to be a place of prayer (John 2:13-16). When He was nearing the time of His crucifixion, Luke says He set His face to go to Jerusalem, walking *ahead* of His disciples (Luke 19:28), knowing that certain death awaited Him. In the garden of Gethsemane, He refused to back away from submitting Himself to the will of His Father saying instead, "Not my will, but thine be done" (Luke 22:42). What a contrast to His disciple,

Peter who was so quick to deny Him because he was afraid of what the crowd would say. We can be loyal to Jesus because we know that when the going gets tough, He will not turn and run. He will stand up to the bullies of this world. He will not suffer religious bigotry to overshadow His love for us.

Furthermore, our loyalty to Jesus is supported by the fact that He was a man of *compassion*.. Some folks may be courageous but their courage is informed by insensitivity to others. Such folk do not really deserve our loyalty. But the fact that Jesus combines courage and compassion reaching out to touch the afflicted, even the contagious disease of leprosy, beckons our loyalty (Mark 1:40, 41). His compassion is seen in the feeding of the multitudes because they were hungry (Mark 5:34). If He was sensitive enough to see that these people were starving and needed food; if He stopped His busy schedule to feed them, does He not deserve loyalty? He wept with His friends at the tomb of Lazarus (John 11:35). He said, "I am the good shepherd. The good shepherd lays down his life for the sheep" (John 10:11), and He did just that. These attributes of Jesus were not lost on Peter. Even though the disciples apparently expected Jesus to be crowned as king in Jerusalem, Peter knew Jesus to be a person filled with compassion. This may have been one of the reasons Peter offered to die on His behalf. One who was as compassionate as Jesus deserved to have others die on His behalf. Peter's passionate expression that he was willing to die for Jesus should remind us to be thoughtful and not glib in expressing loyalty to God. We sometimes do this in singing. Our songs are not always genuine expressions of our true inner feelings. For example, we may sing of our desire that God would order our steps, but as soon as our steps are ordered permitting a little trouble to come our way (Job 1-2; 1 Peter 1:6), we squirm and begin to question God's wisdom and love for us. We sometimes sing "All to Jesus I surrender" but refuse to give up the bitterness we feel toward a brother or sister. Not that we should not sing such songs, but as we sing we should examine our hearts and commit ourselves to live up to what we sing. God is not impressed with our outward expressions of loyalty when there is no inner dedication to do His will.

Loyalty Will Be Tested

Our loyalty to anyone opens us up to various trials. Loyalty is not determined by how we respond when things are going well. Loyalty is forged in the midst of struggle. How do we respond when one to whom we have pledged loyalty is no longer the favorite of the world? Do we turn against him or her? Our loyalty to Jesus must lead us to prayer in the time of trial. When Jesus was the in the garden of Gethsemane, Jesus encouraged His disciples to spend some time in prayer with Him in His time of trial. When our loyalty is tested, we must pray because it is this turn to prayer that keeps us from falling into temptation (Luke 22:40). Apparently, the loyalty of Peter, James, and John was not deep enough to keep them awake and watchful in Jesus' time of trial. The fact they could not pray meant that, at this time the spiritual depth which is needed for true loyalty, was lacking. When we do not pray either before or during our comrades' trials, we set ourselves up for failure of nerve in time of need. This lack of prayer means that when Peter faced the test of his loyalty, he could not stand. Since loyalty develops intimacy with another, Peter refused to follow too closely. Matthew 26:58 tells us that Peter "followed afar off." Many of us fail in the time of our test for loyalty. Loyalty requires a deeper courage than many of us are able to muster. This is why Jesus told him to pray. Your loyalty will be tested. Jesus is very clear that in this world people will seek to turn us from Him. Many things in the world will seek to pull us away and attempt to convince us to betray our God and Lord.

Circumstances in which we find ourselves sometimes lead us to become disloyal to our friends. Peter was afraid to be identified with the man who now was being accused of treason. So often the fear of being identified with the defeated leads us to disloyalty. In this case, Peter denies the Lord three times. Isn't it amazing how, when we are afraid, even persons of no consequence can lead us to deny our loyalty? In this instance, it is a doorkeeper who asks Peter, "You are not one of his disciples, are you?" (John 18:17, NIV). There is a certain ring of accusation in the way the doorkeeper phrases the question. It is meant to evoke a feeling of guilt and shame in Peter. "You are a follower of this criminal. Are you? Not you too. You look too smart to be one of those Jesus freaks. You are not one of them are you?" We may hear others say, "I would expect so and so to be involved in this. But you? I am disappointed." This way the question is asked is directed at the heart of Peter's commitment. It is meant to make him look foolish. It asked to force him into a denial. The world would place you in a situation where your positive response would leave you looking foolish. How many of would still hold on even the face of being shown how foolish our attachment to Jesus looks? At other times, we know that confirming our loyalty could cost us our comfort. Look at Peter standing around a fire along with others to warm himself in the cold of the early morning. Look at Peter, safe within the warm haven of the court that housed his condemned friend. If ever there was a time to affirm his loyalty to the Master, it was then. But fear, oh this sinister fear which clouds the mind and fetters the spirit, got the best of this man. Peter seems to want to disappear among the crowd. His cold was more than physical. He had developed a spiritual cold called fear. He sought warmth among people who could offer him no warmth. His loyalty suffered not only because he was afraid but his fear of being alone in the cruel throng of the people. He needed to identify with the group and be less transparent in his loyalty. Is it not amazing how many times we give up our loyalty because we long to belong? How our desire to be with the "in group" leads us to betray even our inner convictions and, consequently, our loyalties. Once we break loyalty, we often turn to rationalizing. Some of us claim that the reason we betray friends and leave our soul friends out to hang is because there is greater good to be gained. Oh, how religious people sometimes convince themselves that lack of loyalty is for the good of the kingdom of God. Was it not Jesus who said that "the day will come when those who kill will claim that they are doing the will of God" (John 16:2). But much more than that, the road from disloyalty leads downward. When disloyalty takes hold of our heart, the next step in its distorted logic is to lie, once, twice, and in the case of Peter, thrice. Once he has decided his intimate reality, where else could he go? Once many of us start down this path, we are the alcoholic who takes that one drink. Peter lied. First, he claimed he did not know his best friend of three years. Second, he insisted that he has never been with Him. Third, he embellished his lie by saying that he had never set his eyes on this man (John 18:25). He lied again and the rooster began to crow. Look at the way his disloyalty led him to break God's law and the rules of friendship. He failed the test of loyalty. Peter's loyalty had been tested and the man failed three times. Is there not a lesson here for all of us?

In this life, we will be tested. Surely opportunities will arise and temptations to sin against our Master and to deny Him will come. The world will challenge our faith. Concerning offenses that cause us to stumble, Jesus said, "Such things must come" (Matthew 18:7, NIV). He also said that in the world we will have tribulation (John 15:18-21), meaning we can expect persecution because of our identification with Him. But the question is, will fear of tribulation be our opportunity to affirm our loyalty to Jesus or a time when we deny Him because we want to belong with the crowd around the comforting fires of the world?

When Your Loyalty Fails

If, like Peter, your loyalty fails you, even if you're just afraid that your loyalty may fail you in trying times, Jesus tells us that the best antidote for failing during trying times is to pray. When our situations get the better of us and temptation to do evil becomes strong, we must turn to prayer. When difficulties challenge our faith, the best preparation is to pray. Prayer draws us closer to God and fortifies our loyalty and prepares us for the test. In prayer, we confess our weakness to God and reach out for His power. Just as Jesus extended His hand to Peter when he was sinking (Matthew 14:28-31), so the Lord reaches out to any who confess their need for Him and trust Him to help them, which is what faith is. The writer of the Book of Hebrews tells us that the person who comes to God must believe that He exists and that He rewards those who earnestly seek Him (Hebrews 11:6). When faced with temptation, too often we do everything but seek Him in prayer. Failing to pray is what led to Peter's sin of denying his Lord. Filled with remorse, the sinning disciple went out and wept bitterly, doubtlessly condemning himself for going back on his own word.

Renewal of Loyalty Is Possible (21:15-19)

Disloyalty is the breaching of the connection between us and our Master. But with God, no breech is irreparable. After Jesus was resurrected, He sought out Peter. You see, though we may be disloyal, the Lord will never turn on us. The setting for the renewal of Peter's loyalty was the seashore of Lake Galilee. Having returned to Galilee from Jerusalem, Peter persuaded several of his fellow disciples to go fishing Thomas called "Didymus" meaning "the Twin," Nathaniel from Cana, the Zebedee brothers James and John, plus two unnamed disciples; seven in all. How our own failure can lead us to draw in others. Sometimes we draw in others so that we may feel secure in the fact that others have also done what we have done. What prompted them to go fishing? Had they become discouraged and disillusioned about their future since Christ was no longer physically present with them? Were they short on money and went fishing to replenish their funds? Were they simply taking some time for relaxation and refreshment until the other four disciples arrived so they could meet the Lord at the mountain as He had directed? (Matthew 28:16) Was their loyalty also shot? Whatever the case, the Lord sought them out with the intention of healing their hearts broken by disloyalty. For it was not only Peter who had denied the Lord.

We are told that when they went out to fish, they fished all night and caught nothing. How could they? They had breeched the relationship with the fountain of nature. They had turned from the true Son that enlightened the sun. When we betray our loyalty to the Lord, we make our toil fruitless. Our fruitfulness is always the result of the presence and grace of God. Yet even this fruitless labor on the part of the disciple was the Master working to bring them back to themselves. Doubtless, they must have remembered how the Master gave them a boatload of fish in the beginning of their call. Their failure of nerve now served as a lesson in the grace of the Master. In the midst of their fruitless labor, the Master appears and gives direction. To be restored they must listen to Jesus' instruction, "Cast your net on the right side of the boat." While we insist on being disloyal to our Lord, we may toil all we want and still not succeed. We can only be truly successful when our hearts are intimately connected with Lord of the universe. Our renewal will come as we recognize and acknowledge that true "success" comes from the Lord. God does not defines success as the world defines it. Even in the midst of what may *appear* to be failure by the world's standard, God can work glory and fulfill divine purposes.

If disloyalty has taken you out to sea and you find yourself driven by life's tide without a lifeline. Look back to the seashore; there stands Jesus ready to reveal Himself to you. He is a loyal friend. John describes Jesus' presence on the seashore as an "appearance" (John 21:1, NIV) or "revelation" (RSV). In the midst of broken loyalties, Jesus showed up for the express purpose of giving His disciples added assurance. With His death, they thought that He had broken loyalty with them. Did He not tell them that He would never leave them or forsake them? Did He not say, "Where I am there you maybe also?" Here they were. Yes, it is true that they had broken loyalty, but We was supposed to be the Son of God who never fails. Little did they know that the Lord whom they missed was already in their midst. Yes, He has been denied. Yes, He died. Yes, they abandoned Him. His resurrection reaffirms His loyalty to them. Even in all this, His desire to maintain fellowship with them is not dead. Jesus comes to them, who had betrayed Him, and eats with them. Not only did He eat with them, but He prepared fish and bread for breakfast. In many cultures, eating together after a quarrel is an indication that the breach has been cured. Oh, blessed divine loyalty that would not abandon the disloyal. Even in their state, Jesus indicated that His love and concern for their physical needs had not diminished since He had seen them last. See how He humbles Himself and prepares breakfast for those He loved, who in His period of trial would not even speak out a word for Him.

The group had been disloyal to Jesus but Peter, yes Peter, that outspoken disciple, had lied straight-faced that he did not know Him. So when breakfast was finished, the Lord confronted Peter. We cannot be restored if we will not face the Lord and face the fact of our disloyalty. The Master's objective was to restore and renew Peter's loyalty. This must have been difficult since Peter's boasting was not lost on the other disciples. Peter had boasted, "Even

Taylor

if *all* fall away on account of you, I never will" (Matthew 26:33, NIV). So Jesus now asks, "Simon, do you really love me more than these?" Notice that Jesus does not actually call him "Peter" but "Simon." That was his name when Jesus originally called him. At that time, Jesus nicknamed him "Peter" which means "rock." The use of nicknames can be a sign of friendship. Peter must have noticed that he called him Simon and not Peter the "rock." Peter had failed to lived up to his name. In His hour of need, Jesus could not lean on Peter. So this could have been a mild rebuke though not as severe as it might have been. The Lord could have asked him such pointed questions as "How *could* you?" or *Why* did you?" Or even say, "I'm disappointed in you." However, His objective is not to condemn, but to restore. The way to restore our broken loyalty is in returning to the place where we can again show our loyalty.

Three times the Lord asked Peter if He loved Him. Two Greek words for "love"are involved in this dialogue. The word *agapao* is the strongest of the two and refers to love which is self sacrificing. It is love which does not ask for reciprocal love or reward and is not based on the merit of the one who is loved. This is the word John uses when he writes, "God so loved the world that he gave His only begotten son" (John 3:16). Jesus used this word when He asked Peter, "Do you love me more than these?" Since Peter had boasted that he would not forsake Jesus even if others did, the Lord asks Peter to declare if, indeed, he loves Him more than the others. Peter responds using the softer word for love, *phileo.* "Yes, Lord, he said, you know that I have a fondness for you." It is as though Peter could not bring himself to acknowledge love as strong as Jesus suggested. The disciple, doubtlessly remembering his denial of Jesus, had judged himself, concluding that his love for Jesus was not as strong as he had thought. Jesus takes him at his word and based on his answer, Jesus commissions him, "Feed my lambs." Lambs would be those immature believers who were weak and in great need of feeding and protection.

It should be noted that some Bible commentators see no particular significance in the use of the words for love, believing that the writer simply uses two different words for the sake of variety. John uses the word *phileo* on one occasion when Jesus speaks about the Father's love for His Son (John 5:20). Its use in that way on that occasion does not justify minimizing John's use of the two words on this occasion.

The second question from Jesus does not include "more than these," but still challenges the depth of Peter's love. Peter again responded, "Lord, I am fond of you." And the Lord follows this, "Take care of my sheep" (v. 17, NIV).

Asberry

By "sheep" He perhaps means those believers more mature but still very much in need of care. A third time Jesus asks the question, "Simon son of John, Do you love me?" But this time He used Peter's word, *phileo,* or "Do you have a fondness for me? It is as though Jesus is saying, "Since you cannot bring yourself to acknowledge having a *self-sacrificing love* for me, do you at least have a *fondness* for me?" Peter's response is "Lord, you know all things. You know that I have a fondness for you." Again Jesus follows His statement with, "Feed my sheep."

Do the three questions posed by the Lord correspond to the three denials Peter had committed? Perhaps. In the first question, "Do you love me *more than these?"* Jesus had challenged Peter's assertion that he loved His Master more than the other disciples. In the second question, Jesus challenged whether or not Peter had any self-sacrificing love for Him at all, and in the third Jesus had challenged even Peter's fondness for the Lord. These questions caused Peter to face himself, to discover that within himself he was incapable of doing what he wanted to do. This self revealing experience, doubtlessly, helped prepare him for the coming of the Holy Spirit who gave him such power that he would later tell the Sanhedrin council, "Judge for yourselves whether it is right in God's sight to obey you rather than God. For we cannot help speaking about what we have seen and heard"(Acts 4:19-20, NIV).

That Jesus took the time to renew Peter's loyalty is most significant. Had He not done so, the rest of the disciples could have later questioned his apostleship and suitability to use the keys Christ had given him to open the doors of faith to the three people groups Jews, Samaritans, and Gentiles. They could say he had forfeited his right to this role. And perhaps Peter, himself, might have questioned his own suitability for this function. In a sense, Jesus' statement that when Peter is old another would lead him where he did not wish to go could have been an encouragement to Peter. Jesus was referring to the manner in which Peter would die. So Peter is told he will have a second chance to demonstrate his loyalty to his Lord. Tradition tells us that when it was time for him to die as a martyr, Peter requested to be crucified upside down because he did not feel worthy to die in the same way his Lord had died. Jesus then instructs Peter to "follow me" a phrase which in the original Greek language means, "start taking the same road I take and keep on following me." This is an admonition we all need. Can we be loyal to the Master? Can truly love him? Yes! Even if we seem to lack the courage to be loyal in the face of the crowd, Jesus is always there to strengthen us and renew our loyalty when it fails.

Chapter Eight

YOU CAN BELIEVE

John 20:24-29

*But Thomas, one of the twelve, called Didymus, was not with them when Jesus
came. [25]The other disciples therefore said unto him, We have seen the Lord. But he
said unto them, Except I shall see in his hands the print of the nails, and put my
finger into the print of the nails, and thrust my hand into his side, I will not believe.*

*[26]And after eight days again his disciples were within, and Thomas with them:
then came Jesus, the doors being shut, and stood in the midst, and said, Peace be
unto you. [27]Then saith he to Thomas, reach hither thy finger, and behold my hands;
and reach hither thy hand, and thrust it into my side: and be not faithless, but
believing. [28]And Thomas answered and said unto him, My Lord and my God.
[29]Jesus saith unto him, Thomas, because thou hast seen me, thou hast believed:
blessed are they that have not seen, and yet have believed.*

The Book of John focuses on bringing the reader to the point where he or she believes that Jesus is the Messiah. The Apostle John, to whom this book is credited, gives us access to his eyewitness testimony of the life of Jesus Christ the Lord. He seeks to draw us to the "good news," Greek *euangelion* (*eu-*, "good" and *angelion*, "message"), of God revealed in Jesus. Using Hebrew mystical tradition and prevalent philosophical thought, John seeks to have us understand the "Good News," God's incarnation into our world.

Many collections of Jesus' words and deeds were composed in the century after His death, but God uniquely inspired four men to write the Gospels that would bear His authority. The early Christians took time and trouble to discern authentic from spurious records of Jesus' life. The books of Matthew, Mark, and Luke are called the synoptic (one point of view) Gospels because they have much more material in common than any of them has with John.

In the Book of John, he encounters people who refuse to believe Jesus' claim or accept his work as divine. In John 20:31, religious leaders contested Jesus' claim to be the Messiah. Many people did not understand or believe in the mission of Jesus. Believing in all that He said was even difficult for His disciples. Their religious upbringing kept them from understanding Jesus. In fact, it would seem that some of them did not fully believe His words and deeds until after the Resurrection. Take, for example, His conversation with His disciples on the way to Emmaus. Jesus still had to explain things them even after the Resurrection (see John 2:22; 7:39; 12:16; 16:13-16). John was trying help his reader come to terms with the claims of Jesus and thus come to put their faith in Him. He goes to a great length to explain his concepts in such a way that the even those who are not familiar with the tradition of Israel would have their eyes opened. In this passage we see one of the prime examples of the purpose of John's Gospel. Here we see one of the disciples, Thomas, who had walked with Jesus for three years, listened to His teachings and experienced His life, refusing to believe that Jesus had really risen as He said.

After His resurrection, Jesus had appeared first to the woman and then to His disciples. But in all these instances, Thomas was absent. He insisted that he could not believe what he had not seen. Jesus comes to him and tells him that he could believe without seeing. Believing without seeing is not a sign of foolishness but a sign of trust in God. This chapter looks into reasons why we refuse to believe and the fact we can believe the words of the Lord and be blessed.

Skepticism Exposed

"Seeing is believing" goes the adage. Skepticism may be acceptable, but it is a sin when directed towards God. There are many who claim to be realists. These people only believe what they can touch, handle, and smell. In fact, it is our human tendency not believe something of which we are unsure. This keeps us from many troubles. But this tendency can also be a problem for us if we take it too far. When it results in doubt about the promises and power of God, then we are headed for trouble. In our lives, many things arise which force us to reconsider what it is that we have been led previously to believe. Many of us would not believe if, after awhile, our belief is not supported by some experience. So the Lord seems to make sure that we experience little miracles that strengthen our faith. Many things will arise in our lives that may lead us to doubt the validity of believing in God.

The Lord knew that the disciples would have difficulty accepting the fact of Jesus' resurrection, so He arranged numerous events to shore up their faith. The angels rolled away the stone so they could get in to see that the tomb was empty. Angels were stationed at the tomb to convey to Mary Magdalene and the other women that He had risen (Luke 24:4-10). Jesus made a special appearance to Mary Magdalene (John 20:10-18). Peter and John raced to the tomb, found it empty and the unusual configuration of the burial clothes. John concluded He must have arisen (John 20:3-8). Jesus appeared to Cleopas and another person on the road to Emmaus (Luke 24:13-32). He made a special appearance to Peter who became a witness (1 Corinthians 15:5). And He appeared to the 10 disciples in the Upper Room, showed them His crucifixion wounds, and ate fish in their presence (Luke 24:40-43; John 20:19-23). Many times the Lord makes special dispensation to help our faith.

When Jesus appeared to the 10 disciples gathered in the Upper Room, He succeeded in convincing them of His identity and the reality of His resurrected body. But Thomas was not there, so he had missed the blessing of peace bestowed upon the disciples, the demonstration Jesus gave by eating before them, and the breathing on them by Jesus to declare their authority to preach. Part of the problem that many of have in believing God's promises to us is that we are not present with the Lord. That is, we are not spiritually present. Was it because Thomas was not physically present that made it difficult for him to believe or because he had been spiritually absent also? The fact that Thomas still did not believe what the disciples told him, suggested that he had already closed his heart to the spiritual presence. He had allowed himself to be held captive by the physical perception. In spite of all that had transpired between him and the Lord, he could not believe. We know that his friends told him, "We have seen the Lord" (20:25). But none of these events and appearances convinced Thomas that Jesus was alive. Why was Thomas, who had walked with the Lord so long, so skeptical about the reality of Jesus' resurrection? Why do believers who have been beneficiaries of God's goodness continue to display gross doubt about the power of God. We can we not believe? Is our faith so small in spite of all that Lord has done for us? It is people like Thomas who led Isaiah to exclaim, "Lord, who has believed our report?!!" (Isaiah 53:1)

Well, he seemed to have had a personality that always looked on the dark side of things. All we know about Thomas' personality we learn from John's

Keith

Gospel. We meet him when Jesus was preparing to go to Lazarus' tomb (John 11). The disciples had expressed reservation about returning to Judea where the Jews had tried to stone Him. When Jesus informed them He must go anyway, Thomas spoke up to say, "Let us also go, that we may die with him" (John 11:16). This statement revealed Thomas' fatalistic perspective on the outcome of that visit. He fully expected Jesus to die and the disciples to die with Him. Of course Jesus did die, but not the disciples. Many times our lack of belief stems from a pessimistic outlook on life. Fatalism is unbecoming of a follower of Jesus.

The next time we meet the brother is after Jesus announced His soon departure from the world and His reassurance to the disciples that His Father had many mansions waiting for them. He reminded them they already knew the way. Thomas quickly spoke up to express ignorance of how to get to the Father's house, revealing his gloom and hopelessness at the departure of Jesus saying, "We don't know where you are going, so how can we know the way?" (John 14:5) That he had missed much of what Jesus had attempted to convey to them is borne out by Jesus' response: "If you really knew me, you would know my Father as well.... " The brother is gloomy and skeptical.

Skeptics fear being deluded and disappointed. They don't want to appear gullible and made to look foolish in the eyes of their peers. Appearing to be gullible robs them of self esteem. That's why some scientists are so slow to embrace anything that does not meet their test of reliability. They don't want to violate their intellectual sensibilities by accepting something as true when it is not verifiable. Disappointment and pain are associated with having been duped. Of course under some circumstances, skepticism is appropriate. When someone knocks on your door and offers to replace your furnace for $75.00 you have a right to be skeptical. When a quack doctor offers a remedy that promises to cure everything that's wrong with you, you have a right to question the claims. And when a stranger tells you they know how to get you $20,000 if you will just give them $2,000, you ought to close the door in their face.

The question is "How can you tell the difference between a person who is to be believed and one not to be trusted?" Jesus gave a simple answer to that question. You can tell by the *character* or *integrity* of the person presenting themselves. And how can you discern character? By careful observation over a period of time. Jesus said you can tell a wolf in sheep's clothing by their *fruit* (Matthew 7:15-20). When you watch a person's lifestyle over a period of time, their character emerges. The writer of the Book of Hebrews said the same thing when he encouraged believers to obey leaders whose way of life they could observe. He says, "Remember your leaders, who spoke the word of God to you. *Consider the outcome of their way of life*" (Hebrews 13:7, NIV). People who follow media personalities and traveling orators whose way of life they cannot observe set themselves up for great disappointment and disillusionment.

But Thomas had no reason to be skeptical. Ten fellow disciples whose character and friendship were impeccable told him Jesus was alive and had appeared to them. And, doubtlessly, some of the evidence described above had been presented to him. Still he remained steadfast in his skepticism, insisting he had to have irrefutable proof of the Lord's resurrected body before he would believe. "Unless I see the nail marks in his hands and put my finger where the nails were, and put my hand into his side, I will not believe it" (John 20:25, NIV). His statement implies he had been present at the crucifixion and had seen the cruel death the Lord had suffered—the nails, the spear in His side, the burial, and the entombment. And based on all he knew about death and the aftermath of death there was no way in his mind Jesus could be alive. He had seen *Jesus* raise people back to life, but now Jesus was dead (in his understanding) so the accounts he was hearing about Jesus being alive were totally absurd.

Encountering the Master

Jesus obviously overheard Thomas' boast and decided He could not let him remain skeptical. The Lord Jesus was perhaps concerned for two reasons. The Master was concerned about Thomas as an individual. He knew his tendency toward skepticism. In fact, that may have been the reason Thomas was not present when Jesus appeared the first time. He may have been wallowing in unbelief. He was not unlike us, often when our hopes seem delayed or dashed, we build up walls of doubt and negativity. We avoid the company of other believers. How many people in our world have lost the power to believe because they feel like someone on whom they depended has failed them. How many people have walked out of the church or adopted atheism because of the distorted notion that God let something bad happen to them? Yet even these people, Jesus still seeks to win back. Jesus wanted to win Thomas' faith because He loved him and was concerned about him. This divine concern reaches out to all of God's children. Here we see Jesus put his teaching into practice. Did not Jesus say a good shepherd would leave ninety-nine sheep to go into the wilderness to seek the one lost one? The other disciples had seen, heard, and believed Jesus to be alive, but

Thomas was a lone sheep still grappling with doubt, and Jesus was concerned for him. There is a sense here in which the Master uses His own faith in Thomas' future as a child of God to rekindle his faith.

Jesus' concern for doubting Thomas can motivate us to be concerned about the modern doubters. Following the Master, we should be willing to respond gently to people who ask questions about the Christian life. Jesus did not say, "How foolish can you be?" Neither did he say, "How many times have I told you to believe." Too many times when we as Christians are challenged regarding our beliefs, we tend to become defensive. But here Jesus says, "Reach and touch me." Many people of our day, especially young people, often have questions about the Bible that may be embarrassing, but it is incumbent upon us who know and believe to respond in love. Sometimes some questions that people ask are filled with skepticism and border on agnosticism. Yet our duty still remains to respond in the spirit of the Lord Jesus. Other times people may ask us questions regarding portions of Scripture which, to the modern mind, do not seem to make sense. They ask for information. In either case, we should do our best to answer their questions and, settle their doubts.

The other reason Jesus wanted to win Thomas' confidence was so that the disciples would present a unified witness as they faced the skeptics of the world. Can you imagine the doubt that could have been raised in the minds of many people when they preached if one of the disciples were to say, "I'm not sure Jesus is alive"? Thomas had eaten with Jesus, slept with Him in the same house, been taught by Him, followed Him all over Palestine for three years, how close can you get to a person to determine their character and identity? If someone this close was not sure of Jesus' identity because he was not sure He had lived up to His prediction to rise again, why should people of the world believe in Him? Thomas' doubt could have impacted the entire apostolic ministry and the future of the Church. So it was important for Jesus to settle Thomas' skepticism.

How Did Jesus Settle Thomas' Doubts?

In the first place, Jesus *appeared* a second time to the disciples behind locked doors. The fact of Jesus' appearance to them inside locked doors testifies to the truth of the Resurrection and the nature of His glorified body. The laws of physics, which prevent humans from going through material are not a barrier to the glorified body. The Apostle Paul wrote that when Jesus returns to claim His people, He will "transform our lowly bodies so that they will be like his glorious body" (Philippians 3:21, NIV). Coming through the walls as He did should have at least gotten Thomas' attention!

In the second place, as He had done the week before, Jesus *spoke peace* to them. Even though "peace" was a common Jewish greeting, Thomas must have recognized the voice as that of Jesus his Master. And hearing that voice should have begun to dispel some of his doubt. Jesus' primary purpose for appearing the second time to the disciples in this way was to deal with Thomas' doubts. Thomas must have sensed the concern Jesus had for him.

Third, Jesus invited him to do what he said he needed to do to believe *handle the evidence* for himself. "Put your finger here; see my hands. Reach out your hand and put it into my side" (v. 27, NIV). We are not told that Thomas actually did what Jesus invited him to do. Apparently the sight was sufficient. Christ satisfied Thomas' *intellectual* struggle. The sight of these wounds must have also satisfied Thomas' *emotional* doubt, for now as he looked at these wounds, he could remember Jesus saying He was giving His life a ransom for many (Mark 10:45). The reality that Jesus had shed His blood and offered up His life for Thomas could not entirely escape him even though the full meaning of Christ's atoning sacrifice might not have been theologically systematized as it would become later. The sight of those wounds must have melted Thomas' pride and sense of superiority to the other disciples whom he thought were gullible.

In the same way, reflecting on the suffering of Christ can still have a profound impact on people today, especially when we realize what He has done purely out of love for us with there being absolutely no merit in us. Surely, that is why the Lord directed the bread and cup of the communion table to be a time of remembrance. He wants us to reflect and meditate on His suffering for us so that we might, in the midst of an unbelieving world preoccupied with its cares, maintain a vital sensitivity to the meaning of the Cross and be motivated to love and serve Him. Likewise, when an unbeliever takes time to gaze at the Cross of Calvary and realizes that Jesus had done nothing to deserve the cruel treatment He received. When an unbeliever ponders that His death was to pay the sinner's debt for violating the holiness of his Creator, his heart melts at such love. He cries out, as the Philippian jailer, "What must I do to be saved?"

Jesus was perhaps mildly rebuking Thomas because he had not believed the witnesses who told him Jesus was alive. He may have even been upbraiding him for his doubting personality displayed throughout his association with the Lord.

He encouraged him to *believe.* To believe, in the biblical sense, is to place confidence in something or someone to the point of entrusting yourself to it (Genesis 15:6; Numbers 14:11; Matthew 27:42; Mark 1:15; John 1:7, 12; 2:23; 3:16, 36; 5:24; Acts 16:31; Romans 3:22; 10:9; 1 John 5:1, 5, 10). It is not merely to give intellect assent exercise as some people erroneously think. To believe in the trustworthiness of an airplane is to board it. To believe in the trustworthiness of a dollar bill is to present it as payment. To believe in Jesus Christ is to place confidence and trust in Him so passionately that you commit your life to Him and are prepared to do what He directs. Unfortunately, some people present the way of salvation in such a way that people could conclude that to believe is merely to give intellectual assent to Jesus Christ with no expectation that they will need to change their lifestyle. While salvation is a free gift which cannot, in any way, be merited or earned by good works (Ephesians 2:8-9), the evidence of genuine belief is a changed lifestyle a life of obedience to the Lord Jesus (Ephesians 2:10).

Belief Rekindled (v. 28)

When presented with the evidence, Thomas exclaimed, "My Lord and my God!" With this exclamation Thomas let it be known that his doubts were over, his skepticism had vanished. He could say like the songwriter, "Praise God the doubts are settled, for I know, I know it's real." Thomas' words, "My Lord and My God," indicate that he recognized the identity of Jesus. In some respect, Jesus was the same person he had known before His death and resurrection, but his regard for Jesus has deepened. To Thomas, Jesus has demonstrated His *divinity* beyond the shadow of doubt. His statement is one of the clearest affirmations in Scripture when a human being attributes deity to the Lord Jesus. He calls Jesus, my *God.* And there is no indication that Jesus rebuked him for this declaration. He accepted this statement from him because it was true. Jesus is God in the flesh, not just the "Man upstairs." Some may regard Him merely as a great Teacher, or a great Example, but Thomas unmistakably regards Him as God.

John, the writer of this Gospel, likewise regarded Jesus as divine. He referred to Him as the Word which was in the beginning with God and *was* God (John 1:1). John goes on to say that this Word became flesh and made His dwelling among us (1:14). He adduces several witnesses in his Gospel, all of whom testify in some unique way to the divinity of our Lord. He cites the testimony of John the Baptist who says, "Behold the Lamb of God who takes away the sin of the world" (John 1:29, NIV). He records Jesus turning water into wine, a feat no ordinary person could do, showing His control over the natural world (John 2:1-11). John records the testimony of the Samaritans who concluded on the basis of the woman's testimony, but more importantly after hearing Jesus themselves, that He "really is the Savior of the world"(John 4:42, NIV); the healing of the man at the pool of Bethesda (ch. 5); the feeding of the 5,000 (ch. 6); Jesus walking on the water (ch 6); the healing of the man born blind (ch 9); the raising of Lazarus from the dead (ch. 11); and, of course, Jesus' own resurrection (ch. 20); and instructions to the disciples who miraculously caught 153 fish (John 21:1-11). All of these miracles by Jesus point to His divine identity and support His claim that He came from God and bears a unique relationship to the Father. Unless Jesus is God we have no salvation, His sacrifice on the cross has no value, His intercession for us is a farce, and our hope of eternal life is a delusion (1 Corinthians 15:12-19).

Blessing of Believing

Jesus pronounced a blessing upon all those who have not seen His wounds and yet have accepted the message that He died and rose again. He said, "Blessed are those who have not seen and yet have believed." By this Jesus affirmed that it is indeed possible to accept the testimony of others concerning His death, burial, and resurrection. If this were not so, Jesus would have to personally visit each would-be believer, show them His wounds, to convince them of His reality. As it is, the Holy Spirit uses the preached Word to convict sinners of their sinfulness and need for a Saviour as Jesus said the Spirit would (John 16:8). The blessing bestowed is the transformation of the believing person into a child of God to experience the forgiveness of all sins and His on-going presence for empowerment to do the will of God. But it's more than that. The child of God has the promise that one day Jesus will return, transform these weak earthly bodies into bodies that can occupy and function in glory (1 Corinthians 15:35-57), and permit us to forever live with Him.

Chapter Nine

YOU CAN DEPEND ON GOD'S PROMISES

Numbers 13:17-20

When Moses sent them to explore Canaan, he said, "Go up through the Negev and on into the hill country. [18] See what the land is like and whether the people who live there are strong or weak, few or many. [19] What kind of land do they live in? Is it good or bad? What kind of towns do they live in? Are they unwalled or fortified? [20] How is the soil? Is it fertile or poor? Are there trees on it or not? Do your best to bring back some of the fruit of the land." (It was the season for the first ripe grapes.)

Numbers 14:1-3

That night all the people of the community raised their voices and wept aloud. [2] All the Israelites grumbled against Moses and Aaron, and the whole assembly said to them, "If only we had died in Egypt! Or in this desert! [3] Why is the Lord bringing us to this land only to let us fall by the sword? Our wives and children will be taken as plunder. Wouldn't it be better for us to go back to Egypt?"

Numbers 14:11

The Lord said to Moses, "How long will these people treat me with contempt? How long will they refuse to believe in me, in spite of all the miraculous signs I have performed among them?"

Numbers 13:17-20—The Children of Israel, rescued from the armies of Pharaoh, given the Law at Sinai, and sustained in the wilderness, have now come to their appointed destination. The Lord has led Israel to the southern outskirts of the land of Canaan (the Promised Land) to a place called Kadesh Barnea. It is from this place that Moses is told to send spies into the land (v. 2). Moses sent one spy from each tribe. Each spy was a leader in his respective tribe. These spies were to look for specific things. They were told to bring back information about the people (strong or weak), the towns (walled or not), and the land (fertile or not). They were asked, if possible, to bring back a sample of the "fruit of the land."

Numbers 14:1-3—In this section, the spies have returned and given Moses and the Children of Israel a mixed report. They mentioned that the land was "flowing with milk and honey," and they brought back proof. But there was one obstacle, the people of the land were perceived as "giant size." In other words, the inhabitants of Canaan were big. They were giants. Ten of the spies were pessimistic, while Caleb and Joshua believed they could take the land. Caleb said "We should go up and take possession of the land, for we can certainly do it" (v. 30).

The pessimistic report wins the consensus of the people and they complain to Moses and Aaron. They proclaim that it would have been better for them to have remained in Egypt than to die in the wilderness. In verse 3, they question the intention and integrity of God.

Numbers 14:11—The Lord spoke to Moses about His growing impatience with the people's unbelief. With all the signs performed to bring them to this place, they still had no faith.

The sending of the spies was a test for Israel. Moses sent them to gather information. God sent them to see what they would do with that information. God had already told them that the land was flowing with milk and honey and that people lived there (Exodus 3:8, 17). He had told them that He would give them this land that He swore to Abraham, Isaac, and Jacob (Exodus 6:8; cf. Genesis 15:18; 26:3). The question is, would Israel trust God to keep His promise? God had delivered them from Egypt, fed them in the wilderness, given them the law, and correctly described the land. Did God bring them to Canaan to break His promise? Of course not!

The land was an act of God's grace. Man's response should have been simple faith. The ten spies and the Children of Israel were not able to see the obstacles in the right perspective. They had the perspective of man, "We were in our own sight as grasshoppers and so were in their sight" (13:33). They needed the divine perspective, like Caleb, "We are well able to overcome it" (13:30). Because of this act of unbelief, no one from this generation, except for Joshua and Caleb, entered the Promised Land.

God's Promise Is Trustworthy

The land which Israel was about to take possession of was promised to their ancestors, Abraham, Jacob, and Joseph. Abraham knew, firsthand, that God's promises can be trusted. God's promise of progeny had been realized in the birth of Isaac. God also promised to give his descendants the land and to make them a great nation. It was his trust in the word of the Lord that led Abraham in Genesis chapter 12 to leave his extended family and follow God's direction to a new place. All he had to go on was the promise that God will show him the particular land. Sure enough God did show him the land. This again was sign that God's promises can trusted. In verse 7, when Abraham reaches Canaan, God again promises him that He will give Abraham's children this land as an inheritance. In Genesis 13:15-17, the Lord is more specific and tells Abraham:

"All the land that you see I will give to you and your offspring forever. I will make your offspring like the dust of the earth, so that if anyone could count the dust, then your offspring could be counted. Go, walk through the length and breadth of the land, for I am giving it to you."

It is important to note that God does not make this promise temporal but makes it an everlasting promise. By making this gift of the land to Abraham's children "forever," God grounds it in the divine nature. When God says that a promise is everlasting, the only way it can be so is if it is grounded in the very nature of the One who promises. Here God does not put a limitation on this gift. This reminds one of Paul's phrase, "The gifts and calling of God are without repentance" (Romans 11:29). When the Hebrew word *ola* is used as used here, it means that as sure as God can be trusted, this word coming out of the mouth of God can be trusted. It will hold for all eternity.

Though God's promises are eternal, the human beings to whom they are made are not eternal but temporal. Thus it seems that God needs to reiterate the divine promise to every generation. God's promises can be trusted even when we are not trustworthy ourselves. One would think that God would wait until there was a child who was as faithful as Abraham to continue the promise. But God came to Jacob the deceiver and the thief with the same promise. The promise made to his grandfather is restated to Jacob in a dream (Genesis 28:13-17). In this dream, the Lord appears to Jacob at the top of a ladder. The Lord tells Jacob that He is going to give the land, in which Jacob is now sleeping, to Jacob and his descendants. The Lord restates the promise He gave to Abraham almost verbatim. The only difference is the Lord promises to be with Jacob until the promise is fulfilled. The Lord says, "I am with you and will watch over you wherever you go, and I will bring you back to this land. I will not leave you until I have done what I have promised you" (Genesis 28:15, NIV). There are three interesting words used in this powerful promise of the Lords's involvement in verse 15. The Lord says He will "watch over" Jacob. The word for "watch over" is *shamar* meaning "to guard, keep or protect." The Lord promises Jacob His protection. Then He says He will "bring you back" the Hebrew word is *shuv* meaning to "return or go back." The Lord promises to bring Jacob back to the land. The last promise is the promise of the Lord's presence. The Lord says, "I will not leave you" the Hebrew word is *awzav* which carries the idea of abandonment. The Lord has promised that He will not abandon Jacob but will be with Jacob until the promise of land is fulfilled. The promise that is most important to the text in Numbers is the promise of the return to the land. The descendants of Jacob were at the threshold of the land of promise. What will they do? Even when it seems that the promise which was made to your ancestors has failed; even when you have been removed from it for hundreds, yea thousands of years, the same Lord who promised will still come to you to fulfill the promises made. God is trustworthy.

Look at ways through which God sought to make sure that divine promises made will be fulfilled. While they were in foreign a land, Joseph hears his father narrate the promise God made Genesis 48:3-4. Here we see Jacob exhibiting trust in his old age with a clear believe that even after he dies God's promise to give them the land of Canaan will be kept. This belief in the trustworthiness of God's promises is carried on by Joseph. Joseph, on his death bed, shares with his family that God would take them out of Egypt to the land that was promised to Abraham, Isaac, and Jacob. The Lord God reveals the promise to Moses in order to use him as Israel's deliverer. The many references to the land of promise shows that these patriarchs and matriarchs trusted implicitly in the faithfulness of God.

God is always looking for someone to use to fulfill promises made to our ancestors. The Lord appears to Moses (Exodus 3:8) in the burning bush and tells Moses that the cries of the people of Israel have been heard and that the God of their ancestors has come down to deliver them. Moses is further told he will take them to a land that, for the first time, is described as "flowing with milk and honey." In this divine/human conversation, God explains to Moses that other people still live in that land. In Exodus 6:8, the Lord reveals to Moses that this land was promised to the patriarchs and tells Moses that this land will be given to him and his people. The land is again spoken of as: (1) flowing with milk and honey; (2) being occupied by various peoples; (3) the promise to Abraham, Isaac, and Jacob; (4) and God's promise to drive out the inhabitants of the land.

The deliverance of the Children of Israel from Egypt by the Lord's mighty acts and the description of the land as the land of promise flowing with milk and honey set the stage for the drama that takes place in the Book of Numbers. Not failing to mention the sustaining of Israel in the desert and the giving of the Law at Mount Sinai these experiences should factor into Israel's decision-making process. Now at the doorstep of the Promised Land, Israel must decide if the God who delivered them from the land of Egypt can deliver the land of Canaan to them.

Affirming God's Trustworthiness

As Israel camps at Kadesh Barnea, Moses is commissioned by God to send spies into the land. These spies are chosen, one from each tribe. Each spy is a leader within his respective tribe. So God has Moses send the leadership of the tribes into the promise land. Once in the land, they were to bring back specific information about the people, the towns, and the fertility of the land. The scouts remained in the land for 40 days. This is significant because 40 days seems representative of a period of testing, cleansing, or instruction. The rain lasted 40 days and nights to cleanse the earth of its wickedness (Genesis 7:12). Moses twice fasted for 40 days on Mount Sinai. The first time he received the Law (Exodus 24:18 instruction). The second time was for God to forgive the sin of Israel (Exodus 34:27 cleansing). Jesus fasts for 40 days for a period of testing by the devil (Matthew 4:2 and Luke 4:2). Nineveh had was given 40 days to repent by the prophet Jonah (Jonah 3:4 cleansing). And before His ascension, Jesus instructs the disciples for 40 days (Act 1:3).

In every generation, leaders are needed who will affirm God's trustworthiness. God sent leadership to the Children of Israel who believed in the promise and were willing to lead them to the land of promise. But not all leaders bring back the kind of report which affirms God's trust. When the leaders of Israel in the desert were sent, they brought back not a report of God's faithfulness in providing them with the Promised Land but reports implying that God was unfaithful. But watch how trustworthy God is. God did not lie to them. They had already been told that there were inhabitants. They were told the character of this people. God had told them that even though these groups of people were the most powerful in their time, the divine glory would go before them and drive out these inhabitants. God had also said that the land was "flowing with milk and honey" meaning that it was fertile. If they had used their inner eyes, the question would have been: "How would they see?" not "What do they see?" What would be their report? How would it impact what God had already told them? If the tangible evidence contradicted God's word, what would they believe? Would the leaders of the tribes lead their people in faith and victory or in fear and defeat? Could they be trusted to follow the instructions of the Lord, or would they lean to their own understanding? All 12 of the spies confirmed what the Lord had said concerning the land. Numbers 13:27 records their affirmation that the land was flowing with milk and honey. They brought back the fruit of the land to prove it. They even confirmed that the land was occupied by various inhabitants. But after this the report becomes flawed. Ten of the spies felt that the people occupying the land were too strong for Israel to fight. They mentioned that the people were powerful and their cities were large and fortified. They also drew special attention to the descendants of Anak, the Nephelium translated in some Bibles as "giants." The Nephelium refer to the sons of Anak. The King James Version translated this word as "giants." It is unclear who these people were and whether they were related to the Nephelium in Genesis 6:4. Who were great warriors. Whoever they were, the 10 spies had convinced themselves that even with the help of God, they could not defeat them. For these scouts, the stature of these people alone created enough fear to overwhelm their belief in the trustworthiness of their God. They had once expressed their faith in God's power. But now their fears gave birth to the questions: "Can the Lord deliver these powerful people into the hands of the Children of Israel? Can the Lord be trusted to deliver on His promise?" Note that the 10 spies did not deny that the land was flowing with milk and honey. But their concern was that the people of the land were supposedly too strong and too big for Israel to beat them. It did not seem to matter that God had sworn by divine holiness that they would inherit the land. Here we see a group of people who had lost their divine perspective. God said to them, "I have chosen you and treasured above all the nation of the earth," but they insisted on seeing themselves as unworthy. God said, "You are mine, I will make you great and put your fear in all your enemies." They said, "We are like insects" (grasshoppers). God said, "You shall have victory," and they said, "We pray instead to be devoured by a predator." God said, "You shall be victorious;" they insisted on being the victim of their own perception. Instead of viewing this circumstance as another opportunity for the Lord to use them to show His heavenly power, they doubted the strength of the Lord. Instead of seeing their circumstance as God saw it, they insisted on seeing it as an insurmountable object in their path. How faith is vanquished by fear instead of the other way around. The willingness to trust in the promise of the Lord and stay with the direction of heaven is connected, no doubt, to our inner state. The unwillingness to do so is connection to our perception of reality and who we are. Life's situations may cause us to want to distrust the promises of the Lord or may cause us to develop emotive and spiritual hardening which then distorts our faith. What is needed in a circumstance like that is the clear-headed articulation of faith in the promise of the Lord God of Hosts. We see that before this negative report was heard, Caleb had already made a positive statement about taking possession of the land. In Numbers 13:30, we are told that Caleb said, "We should go up and take possession of the land, for we can certainly do it." The statement that Caleb made was a declaration of faith. Within that declaration was a sense of urgency or immediacy. Caleb was calling for Moses and the people to go forward and take the land; it did not matter who inhabited it. Israel could take the land that the Lord promised to her not because of her strength or righteousness but because God the Creator of the heavens and the earth has promised it. Their victory was in the Lord mighty in battle.

Effect of Negative Perception of God's Trustworthiness

Now the people would be put to the test. Which report would they believe: the negative report or the positive report? Would the people remember how the Lord had delivered them from Egypt, sustained them in the desert and had promised to drive out the inhabitants of the land? Unfortunately, they believed the report of the fearful spies. They saw themselves as the 10 spies saw them, as grasshoppers. The reaction to the negative report is recorded in Numbers 14:1-3. The people cried all night and grumbled against Moses and Aaron. They wished to have died in the wilderness or remained in Egypt. This statement is a far cry from the statement made after crossing the Red Sea in Exodus 14:31 which says: "And when the Israelites saw the great power the Lord displayed against the Egyptians, the people feared the Lord and put their trust in him and in Moses his servant." At Kadesh Barnea, the tables are now reversed; the people fear the inhabitants of Canaan more than they fear the Lord. The ultimate statement to that effect is in Numbers 14:3. In this verse, the Children of Israel question the integrity and the intention of the Lord. The Lord had promised to bring them to a land flowing with milk and honey. He had promised to drive out the inhabitants. Now the people question all of this, and ask if the Lord had brought them out into the wilderness to die. They even decided that they did not want God's chosen deliverer. They would choose someone else to lead them back to Egypt. No doubt one of the cowardly spies.

This questioning of the Lord's integrity and intention happened once before, in the garden of Eden. The serpent questioned God's integrity. He flat out called God a liar and said if Eve was to eat of the tree she would become like God. Therefore, God was holding something back from Eve and her husband. God was insecure. The bottom line was that God could not be trusted! Eve, duped by the serpent's reasoning, disobeyed God's prohibition. Then Adam followed suit. There are many similarities with the Children of Israel at the doorstep of the land of promise. Again the Lord's word is challenged. The Lord said He would deliver Canaan into the hands of the Children of Israel. The 10 spies claimed that the inhabitants are unbeatable. The Lord's integrity is now questioned. The people say that the Lord has brought them into the wilderness to die. Lastly, disobedience to the word of God is enacted. They now want to chose a new leader to take them back to Egypt instead of going forward to possess the land. The differences in these two tragic stories is that Adam and Eve were given a prohibition, told not to do something. The Children of Israel were given permission to do something: Take the land! Eve was deceived by the reasoning of the serpent. The Children of Israel's faith was challenged by the report of the 10 spies. Unfortunately, the outcome would be the same. God's judgment would fall.

One last effort was made by Joshua and Caleb to avert calamity that was sure to come. As Moses and Aaron lay prostrate on the ground, Joshua and Caleb appealed to the people. They tore their clothes (Numbers 14:6) and asked the people not to rebel against the Lord. Joshua and Caleb plead with them not to fear the people of the land saying, "Their protection is gone, but the Lord is with us. Do not be afraid of them" (Numbers 14:9b, NIV). Again the people rejected words of faith and wisdom and thought to stone Joshua and Caleb. Then the Lord Himself, intervenes.

The Danger of Refusing Divine Faithfulness

Refusing to acknowledge divine trustworthiness leads to a downward path of separation from divine favor. Not trusting the divine promise, Adam and Eve were banished from Eden. Not trusting the promise of life, they ran into the arms of death. Refusing divine revelation, they embraced rebellion and risked confrontation with the God. This human tendency to believe that, somehow, God will mislead is repeated here by the Children of Israel.

They would rather believe a report that confirms their fear. If the Lord had not intervened to stop them from stoning Joshua and Caleb, they would have added to their sin of denial that of murder. Look at how the path of sin spirals downward. When people set on this downward path, they are scarcely able to stop themselves. Here we see Moses, who has been an obedient servant of the Lord, put his life on the line for these rebellious people. He stood in the gap between divine judgment and the people. Moses pleads on their behalf and quiets God's anger. In a way, he reduces God's sentence of Israel for her sin. Some have said that if it was not for the prayers of Moses, the servant of God, all of the people would have died that day. But his prayer delivered them. But, having set themselves on a downward path, Moses' prayer could only slow them down. The Lord tells the people that for each day (40 days) the spies spent in Canaan this generation will spend a year (40 years) wandering in the wilderness. No one over the age of 20 will be allowed to enter the land of promise save Joshua and Caleb. The rest will die in the wilderness. The 10 spies who led Israel astray were shown no mercy. They died via a plague in front of the congregation. Yet in all these judgments God does no forget the promise made to their ancestors. The promise stands, for God will prepare their children to inherit the promise. The promise of God to every generation is true. If you do not take a hold of it, God will prepare the next generation to receive it. Even when we disdain the promise of the Lord and judgment is declared, God's mercies still continue and are still available. Our tendency is to believe that if we have confessed our faults, then things will immediately return to normal. Here we see how once the people have heard the judgment of the Lord, they confess their sin. But instead of waiting to get direction from the Lord they try to take the land (Numbers 14:40) on their own. They had not believed the promise of the Lord; now they would not obey the command of the Lord (Numbers 14:45). The promise of the Lord is trustworthy. Israel's problem was a seeming inability to believe in whatever God said. They saw every word of God as false. God said, "I would give you the land." They said, "No you won't." God said, "I would mete out punishment," but they did not believe that God would actually do that for they turned around and disobeyed again. It is amazing that even though God had forgiven them and spared them from death, they still walked in disobedience to the Lord and ran into death by the sword of the enemy. The Lord's judgment had fallen.

God Is Trustworthy

The Lord God is a keeper of His promises. The promises made to

Abraham, Isaac, and Jacob will not fail. Ages may have passed, yet God came to deliver Israel from Egypt because of the promise made to their ancestors, the promise that all those who trust in divine goodness will see the salvation of our God. God is willing to fulfill it. God is the God of truth. God's revelation to Israel as the "I Am" points out God's willingness to be for us what we need God to be for the purpose of our fulfillment. Yahweh reveals He has been shown as Israel's protector and deliverer by bringing her out of Egypt. God is revealed as their provider by providing water to drink and meat to eat where there was none. God was to be revealed a generous God, who says in Joshua 24:13, "So I gave you a land in which you did not toil and cities you did not build; and you live in them and eat from vineyards and olive groves that you did not plant." But for those who will not trust in the promise, God would have to reveal Himself as one who judges sin and rebellion. God will give the gifts promised.

The land was an act of God's grace, as Joshua 24:13 states to the second generation. Israel was about to enter a land that the Lord had already set up for them to occupy. The cities where there, the vineyards were planted, and the soil was fertile for other crops. Like Israel, all we have to do is to act in faithful obedience to the divine promise. We can trust God based on what has already been done. As the

WATKINS

Lord's power was proven for Israel in Egypt and in the wilderness, the same power has been revealed for us. We can take our promised land. Should we not act in faith and obedience? Indeed, we should, regardless of the obstacles before us, for the Lord God is with us. Like Israel, it may sometimes be easy to lose perspective. We may see the obstacles in our way as being bigger than ourselves and even God. From the Israelites we can learn that we can take on divine perspective and see our obstacles as opportunities for the arm of God to be revealed through us. Joshua and Caleb knew this. Joshua and Caleb understood that the God who delivered them from Egypt could deliver Canaan into their hands.

The lesson to be learned is that faithful obedience is required in our walk with the Lord. But to do this, we need to remember what the Lord has done for us in the past. We must rehearse the victories of the past to enable us to go forward to conquer the obstacles before us. Realizing that with every new task, journey, or adventure that the Lord sends us, there will be opposition. There will be those "nay-sayers" who will challenge God's word to us. Our main task is to believe what God has stated regardless of the circumstances, and watch the Almighty rain manna from heaven when we are in a dessert place. Our task is to believe and watch the eternal God part the Red Seas of our lives when we feel hemmed in. The Lord is trustworthy and will keep the promises He has made. God will be the "I AM" in every situation we find ourselves in. The blessing comes through faithful obedience to God's Word or direction. In that obedience, we will find that the obstacles that once opposed us have some how vanished, and we can enter into the fullness of the blessing the Lord intended for us to have. Whatever promise God has made to you and yours, God will keep it. God will not disappoint. "Wait, I say, on the Lord."

Chapter Ten

YOU ARE CHOSEN

Deuteronomy 7:6-11

*For thou art an holy people unto the Lord thy God: the Lord thy God hath cho-
sen thee to be a special people unto himself, above all people that are upon the face
of the earth. [7]The Lord did not set his love upon you, nor choose you, because ye
were more in number than any people; for ye were the fewest of all people: [8]But
because the Lord loved you, and because he would keep the oath which he had
sworn unto your fathers, hath the Lord brought you out with a mighty hand, and
redeemed you out of the house of bondmen, from the hand of Pharaoh king of
Egypt. [9]Know therefore that the Lord thy God, he is God, the faithful God, which
keepeth covenant and mercy with them that love him and keep his commandments
to a thousand generations; [10]And repayeth them that hate him to their face, to
destroy them: he will not be slack to him that hateth him, he will repay him to his
face. [11]Thou shalt therefore keep the commandments, and the statutes, and the judgments, which I command thee this day, to do them.*

The Book of Deuteronomy is about the second time God gives the Law to the people of Israel. In this book, the Law is being given to a new generation. The old generation had died in the wilderness for failing to appreciate the greatness of being chosen by God. The Book of Deuteronomy begins by recounting the reasons for the failure of the past generation in chapters 1-2. After that, the author shows us how God confirmed to this new generation, that they were also chosen by giving them victory over the King of Bashan. Here also we see how Moses who was chosen to lead the people ended his great life. In chapter 4, Israel is warned against idolatry. Israel must serve God, for she has been chosen by God. Chapter 5 is a summary of the Law (the Ten Commandments, which is standard for those whom God has chosen). In chapter 6, Israel is again reminded to love God with all her heart. She must choose God and God alone as the One to trust. Chapter 7 which forms the background to our study, gives some practical instruction as to their behavior when, as God's chosen people, they inherit the land which God promised their ancestors. The verses on which this chapter focuses repeats the special relationship between God and Israel. God chose Israel freely and mercifully.

The freedom to choose who will lead us, the privilege to choose who our friends are, and the freedom to live where we choose is a great thing. It is the essence of our humanity. Though sometimes we do choose wrongly, this ability to choose is what makes us truly human. This also is one of the basic aspects of God's nature, the fact that God chooses, unlike us, with perfect insight. God knows completely who is the chosen. God's choice is perfect, even when it seems to us that the people or persons chosen do not deserve to be. Israel was chosen by God's love and mercy. Abraham was chosen to be the father of this holy nation even though he would fail in some respects. God's faithfulness to the covenant established with Abraham resulted in choosing his seed after him.

God's choice is undergirded by God's faithfulness which we read in the Scripture which heads this chapter. That same faithfulness on the part of God gives each one today an opportunity to be special. What a wonderful realization it is to know that you are special to God. What a privilege! Yes, and what a solemn duty that goes with the privilege!

Why Did God Choose You?

In this passage, Moses answered by the Spirit of God what Israel was thinking. The idea that we deserve what we have because we are good is common in the world. Many people sometimes foolishly apply the same notion to the love of God, believing somehow that God deals in merits. It is not the fact that you are special that made God choose you. The fact that God chose you makes you special. In Deuteronomy 7:7, Moses tells Israel, "The Lord your God did not set His love upon you nor choose you because you were more in number that any other people, for you were the fewest of all people." At another place, Moses said to the people

"Speak not thou in thine heart after the Lord thy God hast cast them out before thee, saying, for my righteousness the Lord hath brought me to possess this land: and for the wickedness of these nations the Lord doth drive them out from before thee. Not for thy righteousness, or for the uprightness of thine heart dost thou go to possess the land: . . . Understand therefore, that the Lord thy God giveth thee not this good land to possess it for thy righteousness; for thou art a stiff-necked people" (Deuteronomy 9: 5a, 6).

Often when we are chosen by God, we tend to think that it is because of some intrinsic goodness that God chooses us. Israel was not different from many of us. Having been told by God that they were special and that God had chosen to favor them above all the nations on the face of the earth, one can see how this would go to their heads. In fact, it did go to their heads. As they went into battle and began to conquer the nations which were before them, it was easy for them to start worshiping their own power. Thus we find Israel constantly falling into idolatry. Many times they began boasting that God chose them because they were so special. In many places, God reminded them where they were when God found them and chose them. Just to know where we were when God found us should be enough to humble us. Many of us forget that before we even began to seek God, we were being sought by God. Every choice which God makes of a human being is based on grace. Yes, even the choice of Israel as a God's people was based on grace, love, and mercy. We cannot boast in ourselves. Our specialness does not derive from who we are or what we have done but from the grace of God. God was trying to keep Israel from the vanity of self-praise or vaunting of themselves which leads to idolatry. If we must boast of our place in the Lord, we should be like David and say, "In God have we made our boast all the day long" (Psalm 44:8). The New Testament warns of that glorying which comes from a sense of self-righteousness (Ephesians 2:9; Romans 2:17, 23). Thank God for choosing us as we are!

If many of us were chosen for who we are, then we will have a cause to boast. But it seems that so often God goes out of the way to choose folks who have no ground for boasting. In fact, Jesus displayed this divine tendency by choosing fishermen instead of aldermen. He choose the weak and the ignored of society to teach the world about salvation whereas most of would have chosen the powerful and the influential. But if God knew that if you were chosen because you are a great speaker, you will have cause to boast about your ability to speak. If God chose you because you have much money, then you boast about your wealth. If God choose you because of your political influence, sure enough, you will boast of your power. But God did not choose you because you were wise, for you would have an occasion to fall into pride. The Master calls us to lay down our pride and to present

Dea Johnson

ourselves naked or with our rags, and God, even our God, will clothe us with mercy. Jesus, just like the God of the Old Testament whom he calls Father, calls poor ones saying to Him, "Follow Me." If perchance they cannot follow because they are too weak, God will carry them. God chooses those who have nothing, that they may find true riches in the divine presence. God chooses even the ignorant, so that through the in-filling of the wisdom of God they may become special. God chooses those who are empty and dry, so that they may be filled from the eternal fountain. So God choose Israel out of all the nations that she may receive grace and become God's treasure. Paul, the apostle, sums this up when he says,

"But God hath chosen the foolish things of this world to confound the wise; and God hath chosen the weak things of the world to confound the things which are mighty, and base things of the world hath God chosen, yea and things which are not, as if they were, that those things which are may be brought to nought" (1 Corinthians 1:27-28).

In whatever state you may have been, or in which you may currently be, God has chosen you to show forth His glory.

Why did God choose you? God wants to make your part special. The psalmist raised the question, "What is man, that thou art mindful of him" (Psalm 8:4), and goes on to observe that God crowned human beings with glory and honor. In Jesus, we find that God chooses to reveal His glory with the very lowly things of life. Jesus was born in a manger, slept in a borrowed room, and had no place to lay his head. Yet, through Him, God wills the world to be saved. God chose you to show forth the abundance of divine mercy and love. This mercy and love is so abundant that it is offered not just to Israel of old or the apostles of the first century, but even to all humankind.

The fact that this choice is grounded in the life of God's own Son puts a special premium on you. You are treasured by God. You are so special in God's sight that your salvation was purchased by the perfect atoning blood of our Lord and Saviour Jesus Christ on Calvary. Though human beings have constantly failed in their attempts to become reconciled with God, God nonetheless continues to choose people who may serve the divine purpose. By becoming a human being of flesh and blood just to bring redemption to us, God shows us how special those who have been chosen by God really are. Their specialness is found in the fact that they have been chosen by God.

Now you are chosen, not because of your merits or because of your good works. This choice is of grace: "But if by grace, then is it no more of works, otherwise grace is no more grace." Being chosen through grace, we under-

R.chardson

stand that all our so-called good merits are nothing or as Isaiah said long ago "filthy rags" (Isaiah 64:6). Because it is given so freely and without our own work, God owes us nothing. If we were chosen because of what we have done, then God is in our debt. But the Bible declares that "God is a debtor to no one." In fact, we are the ones who owe God, yet even in our bankruptcy God has chosen us. We had nothing to bring to the table. Amazing grace! To give a glimpse of this, Paul is saying, "that while we were yet sinners, Christ died for us" (Romans 5:8). Hear, the Divine Master is saying, "I have chosen you." The world has a different way of choosing. It chooses you based on what it thinks it can get from you. But the truth is that if you are chosen for your wealth, when your wealth is gone you are no longer chosen. If you are chosen for your beauty, when you are beyond your prime, you are no longer a good choice. I am glad that God does not choose based on such frivolous human standard or even on what you or I have done.

On What Is God's Choice Based?

The choice of anyone, Israel, the Church, you, or I is based on the very character of God. Several attributes of the God which undergird His choice are revealed in this passage. Moses says, "But it was because the Lord your God loved you." The first ground on which God chooses is love. This love is who God is. God chooses you not according to who you are (see 1 John 4:8). So the question is, "Why did God choose me?" I can answer without hesitation, "Because God loves me." The love of God is greater than any other. It's depth, who can fathom? It's height, who can imagine? It's width, who can comprehend? (Ephesians 2:4) It will abide as the psalmist says, "Forever." God's love never fails (Isaiah 49:15-16). In fact, once God's love is set on you, nothing in the world can alienate that love from you (Romans 8:39). You see? If something can separate you from it, then God's love will find its strength like that of a mere mortal. But God's love is grounded in the eternal nature of God. This is how we know that God can love us even when we do not deserve to be loved. To say, then, that God has loved you is to say that the Divine Self has been given over to you before you even knew that you could breath. Such love which chooses us before we even knew our names. What Love!! This is love which chooses us and accepts us even though we do not deserve it. What love! (See Deuteronomy 7:7; John 16:27; 17:23; 2 Thessalonians 2:16; 1 John 4:16.)

The second ground mentioned here is that this choice is based on God's faithfulness. The Hebrew word for faithful is *a man* **(aw-man).** It means that God is one who builds support for those whom He has chosen. Like a good parent, God's choice includes the power to nurture. Indeed God's choice is firmly grounded, not fickle like that of most human beings. Because the One who chooses you is faithful, you can trust. You can stop worrying and rest in it. God will not choose you today and abandon you tomorrow. That does not mean that God will not deal with our foolishness. As we shall see later, that's far from true. But it does mean that God's choice is permanent. The fact that in this portion of Scripture, we also read that God "kept the oath which God swore to your forefather," also means that God is true to His choice. Hence there is an assurance that God will not abandon the people He chooses.

Benefits of Being Chosen by God

Having been chosen by God, you are now a candidate for God's mercy. You obtain mercy by being chosen. The Hebrew *checed* (**kheh'-sed**) from which the word "mercy" is translated can mean kindness. But it is more than that. It can also include the idea of reproof. So when Moses says that God shows mercy to those who by divine grace have been chosen, it does not mean that what we do does not matter. Rather it means that God forbears from punishing us immediately, giving us all the chances in the world to come to our senses and return to Him. God's has mercy upon those who are chosen. This mercy is more than pity. It is a beautification of the one chosen. This is connected to what Moses says in verse 6. Moses says that God has made you a "treasured possession" (NIV) or "chosen thee to be a special people" (KJV). God chose you so that God can set divine glory upon you.

Second, because God has chosen us, God will ransom us from our troubles. The idea here is that God will sever the chains that bind us. When we are enclosed, the Lord will release us. When we can find no way out, the Lord will make a way. Having been chosen, we are now preserved by divine mercy and love. With regard to Israel, God showed this mercy by delivering them from troubles into which their foolishness plunged them. In the same way, God will deliver you from your troubles, for you are chosen.

Third, God will bring you out of whatever oppression that binds you. Not only has God, by choosing us, released our chains, but God will make sure that we are brought to an open and free space where we can freely serve God our emancipator. As a result of this choice, you can now go out of your cell. It is in this same vein that Jesus reminds us, "So if the Son sets you free, you will be free indeed" (John 8:36, NIV). It is common knowledge that one who has been in darkness for a long time, even after they have left the dark cave, may still feel the after effects of the night in which they were so enclosed. When Moses said to Israel, "The Lord brought you out with a mighty hand," he was implying that God has been the One who gave them direction and is always near. You are chosen, so be sure that God will carry out His plan for you. You are chosen; you shall not be condemned or confined to spiritual narrowness. You are chosen; therefore, you shall escape all the traps of the enemy. When the enemy surrounds you, God will make a way for you to escape. In the time of trouble, your help will not be scarce. God will send His angels with explicit commandment to spring you out of the devil's trap. Surely you know that you have been chosen just as Israel was chosen. You have been sanctified unto the Lord God for great things.

God graciously promised benefits to those who faithfully adhered to the divine Word. God promised Abraham that Israel will be a great nation, and that promise was kept in spite of Israel's perpetual backsliding. Ward Patterson, in *Wonders In the Midst,* asserts "Beginning with the miraculous deliverance from captivity in Egypt, continuing through the years of wilderness instruction in the ways and will of God, and culminating in the conquest of the promised land, God's wonders protected, saved, directed, corrected led, and sustained His people." God repeatedly reached out to the Israelites in love and mercy because they had been chosen to be God's own. The same God has chosen you and will be with you.

Chosen for Responsibility

But you are not just chosen to be a decoration in the temple. Israel was chosen to be a people. In this case not just any people, God's people. Now God calls them a "holy people" even though they continued in their stubbornness. They were to be a congregational unit by the divine call and purpose. Much more than that, they were collectively to be God's attendants. Now they must relate to God as a flock does to a shepherd. Thus, as God's flock, they were to listen and follow God's directions. As God's people they, were to be characterized by a holy lifestyle. Amazing as it may seem, Moses does not say in this passage that they should be holy, but "You are a holy people unto the Lord your God." They have been made holy by the very act in which God chose them. God had pronounced them holy. By divine appointment, they have now been sanctified unto the Lord. As a result of this, they must now intentionally consecrate, dedicate, and commit themselves not to defile but to hallow the name of their God.

Note also that this call to be holy is not directed to them as if they were doing this just to look good, but it is directed to God. They are holy unto the Lord their God. This is important because those who are chosen are not chosen just for themselves but to fulfill God's purpose. There is a place for everyone who is chosen. There is charge to keep for all of us who are chosen. We must prepare ourselves to proclaim the power and the purity of our God. God has sanctified us for a purpose. Our sacred duty, as peculiar persons, cannot be fulfilled by another. When God says to Israel through Moses, "You are a holy people unto the Lord your God," this means that they are no longer responsible to another god. They have been lifted to a position of divine eminence. God's choice always comes with great responsibility. God's choice of Israel meant that a great responsibility lay upon the people to keep God's commandments and to become a holy nation. The Apostle Peter reminds us that under the New Covenant we, likewise, are chosen to be a holy people unto the Lord (1 Peter 1:15-16). Our being chosen lays upon us a great responsibility. Though we did nothing to deserve the love of God, yet in gratitude to this choice, we must respond to God in a certain way. We must meet love with love. We must meet divine faithfulness with trust. We must meet divine mercy with humility. In the later part of verse 9, we read that God is "the faithful God which keepeth covenant and mercy with them that love Him and keep his commandments to a thousand generation." The Hebrew word for the love which we ought to have toward God is *'ahab* **(aw-hab)** or *'aheb* **(aw-habe')** which means to have a deep affection. If we know we have been chosen, we must now act friendly toward God. We are now God's friend. So as the chosen, we are now so intimate with God that whatever we do reaches directly into the heart of God. We have the capacity to wound the heart of God. This passage is continuation of the first commandment, "Thou shall love the Lord thy God with all thy heart." This commandment is always stated as the response of grateful people to God's redemptive activity.

Another principle here is that our love of God in response to God's love and work on our behalf secures a future for us. How does this love of God show forth itself in the chosen? It is revealed in the *shamar,* the Hebrew word for "taking root in God's presence" or "to shine forth." Here, it means to protect the honor of God and to guard it even with our lives. So in general, we must attend to the very character and name of God in such a way that our whole life bears witness to this. Paul warns us in Hebrews 6 that those who are chosen must beware lest they take their choice for granted. There are certain courtesies that every true friendship must observe in order to preserve its integrity. In this case, God is telling those whom He has chosen to regard Him with respect. Reverence and honor firms up a relationship between friends. So also it is between us and God who has chosen us. If we keep the commandments of this friendship, they will preserve and save us from ourselves, from the world, and ultimately from a falling out with God. "To a thousand generations" is just one way of saying for a long time or forever. Having been chosen by God, we cannot afford to hate God or to act hatefully toward our Lord.

As you reflect on the fact that God chose you, meditate on Israel's past history and become aware of the characteristics that will strengthen your relationship with God. At the same time, we must be reminded of those traits in our lives which invite the judgment of God. But in all this, never forget that you have been chosen, you have been set apart for God, and you have been planted in the heart of God. Whatever question you may encounter, God has already anticipated, and, in choosing you, He has already determined the answer to your questions. Whatever your children will face, though you may not be there to answer them, God, who has chosen you, will be there for them. If anyone asks you, just tell them you have been chosen by a mighty and marvelous God. You have been chosen like the Israelites were for a purpose. If you are not yet clear as to what your purpose is, just know one thing, you have been chosen to show the love of God who called you. Tell the world that because God has chosen you, you know that you are God's treasured possession. Tell them that you know that you are not perfect. Tell them that you know that you are not the most wealthy person in the world. Tell them that you know you are not the smartest person in the world. But don't forget to tell them that in spite of all this, you know that you have been chosen by the eternal, sublime, and most glorious God. You now belong to God and nothing in the world can undo the fact that you have been chosen by God (Deuteronomy 7:7). Of all these, do not forget to tell them that you are, indeed, a child chosen and drawing near to God by the way you live. Remember that your being chosen gives you a great responsibility, but by the grace of the God who chose you, you will be able to carry out this responsibility. Amazing grace chooses people like us.

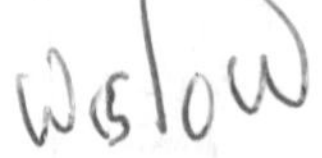